ADVANCE
LEADING FR

"Obi Abuchi has written a much-needed book on the fundamentals of leadership, brimming with timeless principles for today's busy landscape. If you are a leader, I urge and encourage you to not just have it on your shelf but to ensure that this message gets into the core of who you are."
Toye Oshunbiyi, *Founder & CEO, Business Leaders Coach*

"Easy to read and packed with deep insight. It's a must-read for those who want to make a real difference to the people around them and in the world."
Chris Chin, *MD, Curious Learning and author of The Gift of Collaborative Feedback*

"Time waits for no leader. Obi Abuchi knows this. For those leaders who know intuitively that the time is now for a more inspirational, authentic, connected and fulfilling way to lead – this is the book that will affirm that knowledge and uniquely guide the way. For those leaders who don't – this is an absolute must-read."
Niamh Flood, *Group Head of Organisation Capability & Head of HR - Operations, daa*

LEADING FROM YOUR CORE

"In addition to being a most enjoyable read, *Leading from Your Core* is a practical and pragmatic, yet inspiring take on effective leadership in today's world of the unexpected. It is an integral tool to self-mastery and development which, in my view, should be the quest of every single leader today."

Yetunde Hofmann MBA, FCIPD, FRSA, *Board Director, Coach, Speaker, author of Beyond Engagement, Founder of Solaris, and MD Synchrony Development Consulting / The Enjoyable Life Series CIC*

"*Leading from Your Core* holds a mirror to our society, showing us the leadership we have been dealt, forcing us to face our truth, while offering a path to effective leadership that has people at its centre. Thank you, Obi Abuchi, for this much needed lesson and reflection."

Keith Kibirango MCIOF(Dip), *Founder, Abantu Impact Foundation*

"Hugely relatable, insightful, and thought-provoking. I have been recommending it to people even before it is published! The style of writing makes you feel as though you are receiving one-on-one coaching. A must read for all leaders."

Sandy Willoughby, *Consulting Director, NKD Learning*

"An easy and compelling read that cleverly challenges and supports you simultaneously. This is a real handbook for today's real contemporary leaders – I can assure you it will not take you long to finish, but you'll talk about it for so much longer."

René Carayol MBE, *Global Leadership Speaker, Executive coach, and author of SPIKE*

Advance Praise for Leading from Your Core

"*Leading from Your Core* is a transformative leadership book. Obi Abuchi invites you to embark on a courageous journey of self-reflection and self-mastery. Each chapter will challenge you to examine deeply how you lead others. Obi Abuchi provides practical strategies to transform how you lead and live."

Faith Ruto MBA, *Executive Coach, Speaker, and author of Transform Within*

"Do you have a voice inside that sometimes questions how well you're leading? If you're brave enough to read this book, it will help give you the most personal diagnosis to that question, but most importantly you'll come out the other end a much better leader."

Phil Akilade, *CEO, The Business Transformation School and author of Transformation From Chaos*

"Whilst there are many average, good, and even great leadership books out there, Leading from Your Core is the one I challenge all leaders to participate in. Yes, I said 'participate' as Obi Abuchi takes you on a journey. Regardless of your starting place, you will be taught, reminded, and challenged to do better and be a better version of yourself – from the inside out!"

Jasmine Perera, *Life Coach and Master NLP Practitioner with Applied Neuroscience*

LEADING FROM YOUR CORE

"Obi Abuchi has done with his book what few others do when writing about leadership. He explores the whole person, to their core, not just the bits that show up at work."
David McQueen, CoFounder, Q SQUARED

"In this book, Obi Abuchi has started a mindset shift around putting your soul into the authenticity of leadership. His guidance will inspire you and strengthen your character. Stay curious and let Obi Abuchi lead you into a whole new world of leadership."
Sylvia LeRahl, Founder, Membership Fix and author of Hide the Exit

Oct. 2024

May your leadership impact continue to be a light to the world. Stay inspired!

Obi

Col. nov

May your leadership
inspire contrive to
be a lift to the world.
May God speed
CA

The Path to Becoming a Purposeful, Courageous, and Resilient Leader

LEADING FROM YOUR CORE

OBI ABUCHI

Leading from Your Core
The Path to Becoming a Purposeful, Courageous, and Resilient Leader

Copyright © 2021 by Obi Abuchi

ISBN 978-1-3999-0189-5

All rights reserved. No part of this publication may be reproduced, stored in a retrieval system, or transmitted in any form or by any means – electronic, mechanical, photocopying, recording, or any other – except for brief quotations in printed reviews, without prior permission of the copyright holder.

Books may be ordered through booksellers or by contacting:

CORE Leaders International

www.coreleaders.co.uk

Cover design and interior design: Jennifer Stimson

DEDICATION

Mum, I thought I was done after one book,
but in your love and wisdom you encouraged me
to continue to share my insights with the world,
and I am so glad you did.

Thank you for all the incredible love, encouragement,
and belief you have poured into me over the years.

There is no denying what game you were playing.

I love you always.

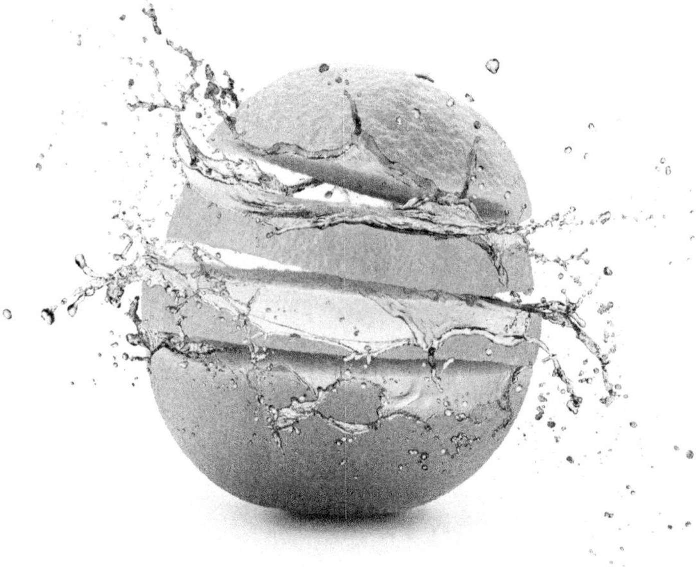

CONTENTS

PREFACE 13

INTRODUCTION - What Game Are You Choosing to Play? 19

PART 1 - Why Having a Strong Core Matters 33

   CHAPTER 1 - It's Costing Us 35

   CHAPTER 2 - What You Really Think About Leadership Matters 51

PART 2 - What a Strong Core Looks Like 61

   CHAPTER 3 - The Audacity to Focus Within 63

   CHAPTER 4 - The Heart of Leadership 83

   CHAPTER 5 - The Currency of Leadership 97

PART 3 - How You Can Develop a Strong Core 113

   CHAPTER 6 - Prepare to Transform 115

   CHAPTER 7 - Align Your Life Around Clear Values 129

   CHAPTER 8 - Live with an Optimistic Worldview 141

   CHAPTER 9 - Cultivate Rewarding Habits 151

   CHAPTER 10 - Nurture Empowering Beliefs 161

CONCLUSION - Walk the Talk 173

EPILOGUE 179

ACKNOWLEDGEMENTS 185

BONUS SECTIONS 189

Crafting Your Life Plan and Leadership Philosophy 191

The Personal Mastery Academy 193

About the Author 195

PREFACE

"We desperately need more leaders who are committed to courageous, wholehearted leadership and who are self-aware enough to lead from their hearts."
- BRENÉ BROWN

Many leaders have lost their way. You could even argue that, around the world, within our political institutions, commercial enterprises, voluntary groups, and religious organisations, very few leaders ever found the path to effective, engaging, and transformational leadership in the first place.

It might sound like an insanely damaging indictment, but I say it soberly. Also, I genuinely don't think most of these leaders intentionally want to be ineffective or diminish their impact. Speaking from personal experience, many of us are either simply looking in the wrong place, have a faulty leadership paradigm, or have poor examples around us.

Let me explain.

My first experience of working closely with very senior leaders in business was a defining one for me. It was a few years after graduating. I had been hired as a train systems engineer and accepted on to the graduate development programme of an engineering and construction firm with responsibility for a multi-billion-pound schedule of improvement and maintenance of the London Underground.

I didn't really enjoy the engineering side of the role, but I was lucky. Only eighteen months into the programme, I secured a six-month placement to shadow the managing director of our sister company.

I attended many key meetings, including some board meetings and one-to-ones, and engaged in various projects with senior leaders and middle managers, on behalf of the managing director. I observed what it was like to be at the helm of an organisation – the power, the authority, the resources at your disposal – and to be completely honest, I didn't always like what I saw.

The managing director, in particular, was extremely intelligent and experienced, yet he had a reputation for berating the life out of those working for him. If he felt someone was incompetent and hadn't done something to his standard, they would know it, along with every other person within earshot of them. He instilled fear into many as he asserted his authority and intelligence.

Preface

Even though I got on well with him, enjoyed our one-to-one conversations, and learnt a ton during the six-month stint, after that experience, I promised myself that if I ever had a chance to lead people – choosing between leading by asserting my authority, intelligence, superiority, and power or from a place of genuine, positive influence – I would choose the latter.

Since then, over more than two decades, I have developed a passion for leadership, grown as a leader, held various leadership positions, and studied some of the best leaders and leadership experts on the planet. I have become fascinated by the difference that truly effective, inspirational, and transformational leaders make to those around them.

I have asked myself:

- What is it that helps them to see the potential in pretty much everyone around them?
- What is it that drives them to inspire and equip others to dream more, think more, believe more, learn more, do more, and become more than they ever thought possible?
- What is it that enables them to earn the deep respect of others and unleash the best in them during the good times and the extremely tough times?
- What have they learnt about the secret of positive influence?

In this book, I will share some of the answers with you, especially because this sort of leadership not only transforms lives and leads to healthy and thriving organisations and communities, but it also creates a better world. And that is something I am desperately committed to.

Now, let me ask you a question. I would really like you to take some time to pause before you answer it: **Is the way you are leading *really* working?**

[I encourage you to pause for a few minutes and take some time to reflect on your answer to that question before moving on.]

When asked a question like that, our minds easily go to the standard metrics for assessing leadership effectiveness:

Business results.
Employee engagement scores.
Share price.
Merger success.
Customer satisfaction scores.
Business transformation.
Sales pipeline.
Revenue generated.
Market share.
Volunteer engagement.

Forget all of that for a moment. I want to take this much further and deeper by considering not only the way you *lead* but also the way you *live*.

What is it like for the people under your influence?

Preface

Is the way you lead enabling those around you, from all walks of life, to truly thrive? Is the way you lead inspiring others to bring the best of themselves – their motivation and talents and creativity and passion – to whatever endeavours they are engaged in? Is the way you live adding tremendous value and meaning to your life and the communities you are a part of? Is the way you live and lead helping you to develop burnout resilience, maximise your energy, and increase your positive impact on the world?

As you will soon discover, this is not merely a book on effective leadership. This book is about helping you step back and courageously look deep within yourself, at your humanity, your life, your vision and values, your worldview, your beliefs, and your habits. It is about helping you examine the foundations of who you really are, so that you can truly live your best life and inspire the best in those you influence – at home, at work, at school, in organisations, and in communities – during the good times and the tough times.

As well as experiencing greater effectiveness and impact in your leadership, the fruits of going on this journey include a clearer sense of purpose and fulfilment, peace amid personal and professional storms, increased mental fitness and fortitude, deeper connections with others, greater alignment with your best self, and the clarity that you are being and living as you were designed to live.

This is a journey that will transform the way you lead from the inside out.

While writing this book, I pulled together some of my most potent leadership insights from over two decades, including my experience of working with, training, and coaching leaders in giant corporations and voluntary organisations. In addition, I interviewed over 60 leaders[1] from a variety of organisations all over the world on the topics of leadership effectiveness, personal mastery, burnout, and resilience. They were extremely generous with their time and honest about their experiences. I am thrilled to share many of their insights and stories, in some cases anonymously, straight from the battlefield and the line of fire, so to speak.

I believe deeply that this book is a stimulating and thought-provoking read that will move you to take action that not only helps you become a more effective, purposeful, engaging, and transformational leader, but also a better husband, wife, dad, mum, friend, son, or daughter.

So, enjoy the journey, take courageous action, and GROW!

Obi Abuchi
September 2021

---

1 In this book, you will sometimes see this symbol ✶ next to someone's name. It indicates that that person is one of the leaders I interviewed.

INTRODUCTION

What Game Are You Choosing to Play?

"To live is to choose. But to choose well, you must know who you are and what you stand for, where you want to go, and why you want to get there."

- KOFI ANNAN

I have had the privilege of working with leaders all around the world, from a range of backgrounds, in various types of organisations, and I have come to the firm conviction that there are only two games leaders play.

And so, to save you the trouble of investing your time reading any more of this book, I will describe both games and make it crystal clear who this is and, even more importantly, is not for.

Is This Book Right for You?

In *177 Mental Toughness Secrets of the World Class*, Steve Siebold describes the different levels at which people live, think, and play the game of life. The model is so relevant for leaders that I often use it when I am coaching them, and I will also use it here to explain Game one. I have adapted the descriptions to a leadership context.

Game one is the **Ego Game**.

The first level of the Ego Game is *playing not to lose*. At this level, as a leader, you are dominated by the fear of failure and not performing well. You are threatened and heavily influenced by the views, opinions, and approval of others. You do a lot of what you do simply to avoid the consequences. It gets you some traction at least.

The next level of the Ego Game is *playing to cruise*. This is where you are all about staying under the radar. You still adopt a fear-based approach to leading and playing the game of life. You see leadership as a position with rewards. You do a lot of what you do for some of the rewards, nothing more. Some would describe this as operating at the level of mediocrity.

The third level of the Ego Game is *playing to improve*. You're really beginning to switch gears here. As a leader, you realise that you can accomplish more than you originally thought. You might even be better than people said you were. You begin to step up and assert yourself more. The rewards, the recognition, and the power also become more appealing, and your commitment to self-interest grows.

The fourth level of the Ego Game is *playing to compete*. This is where you're really focused on making your team, group, or organisation the best because it looks good and delivers more rewards for you. You see your peers as competition. You are acutely aware that leadership comes with rewards, recognition, and power. You love the high that comes from those things, and you want more of it.

I have worked with a lot of driven and 'high-performing' leaders who operate at this level. They have strong beliefs and confidence in their capabilities, but they are still driven by fear, ego, and a scarcity mindset. It's still about what they can achieve. It's still about protecting their reputation. It's still about making a name for themselves. It's still more about asserting their superiority, their intelligence, and their authority. The way they govern, manage, and lead are an absolute testament to self-interest.

The fifth level of the Ego Game is *playing to win*. This is the level where you are no longer merely competing with others but also against yourself. You continue to be plagued by inner conflict but have learnt how to numb it. You have a lust for glory and a desire to ensure you are well out of the league of your competition in results, acquisitions, and performance. For you, leadership is a right, and the power and rewards that come with it are the deserving prize of all your labours.

The shift from level four to level five feels like a phenomenal one to many. After all, you're focused on being your absolute best and achieving the honour, respect, and admiration of others. You have come a long way from not really believing in yourself to believing that you are miles better than the rest, and you have all the rewards and accolades to prove it.

For many leaders, it's only when they get here that they begin to realise they are living outside their values, they have burnt loads of bridges, and they have lost a lot of friends and loved ones along the way. Their own drive for and commitment to self-interest makes it hard for them to trust others because they think they too are only in it for themselves.

That's game one – the Ego Game. So many leaders play that game and love it. Like I said earlier on, they really don't know or believe in anything else.

Sadly, building our life and leadership legacy on the qualities that define the Ego Game only serves to create an unstable foundation, in the way we live and lead, so much so that when the pressures of life and business come our way, they rock us to our very core. More on that in Chapter 1. What's more, **leaders who play the Ego Game, at best, achieve compliance in their people, but they never ever win hearts and minds.**

What Game Are You Choosing to Play?

Game two is a very different game. It is based on a different mindset altogether to the Ego Game.

In this game, you are not consumed with what your people can do for you, but what you can do for them. You're not plagued by inner turmoil and conflict. You're not into putting up appearances or hiding behind a façade. You're not driven by an aspiration to be popular, but by a desire to equip others and help them grow. You're not obsessed with all that is possible for you to achieve, do, and acquire but with the amazing and untapped potential that exists within those around you. You don't see leadership as a right, but as a responsibility.

You recognise that what you *do* as a leader matters far more than what you *say*. You willingly accept accountability for the well-being of the larger organisation, and you fulfil that accountability by operating in service, rather than in control, of those around you. You value connection over control. You value partnership over patriarchy. You value passion over compliance. You value empowerment over dependency.

When you're playing this game, you are about learning, growing, contributing, and expressing yourself. At the same time, you are completely attuned to the needs of those around you and excel at drawing out the best in them for the common good of the organisation, the community, the family, or, indeed, our world. You have learnt how to weaken your inner critic and strengthen your inner coach. **You are committed to intentionally creating an environment that inspires and motivates people to become the best they can become.** You don't get drawn into or feel afraid of what others think because you're not playing the Ego Game.

Nikola Hagleitner✶ describes the leaders who play this alternative game as "the sort of leaders who genuinely want others to have a great life. They walk their talk, live up to their principles, and have clarity about who they are. They recognise that if you lead in a way that is only about results, people follow you because of your authority, but they never respect you as a person."

This alternative game is the **Service Game**. It's all about playing to give, grow, build, contribute, and serve.

Now that you know the two games, please note that this book is only for leaders who have chosen to play, or who want to learn how to play, the Service Game and that game only. This book is for those emerging and seasoned leaders who are committed to channelling their ego for the good and service of others. It is for those leaders who are no longer interested in seeing or promoting leadership merely as a matter of intelligence, superiority, position, or asserting one's authority. It is for those leaders who are willing to do the hard work – and trust me, it *is* hard work – of leading from the inside out.

By the way, if the Ego Game sounds familiar to you,

do not be alarmed. I can assure you, most of us fall into this trap because it's the predominant game that we see leaders play all around us. The key thing is that you commit to playing a different game – the Service Game. No matter what level of the Ego Game you are currently on, playing the Service Game begins with a decision – a decision to lead for the good and service of others, our communities, and our world. If that's your desire, then please do read on.

The Importance of Committing to the Service Game

Why is it so important that you're committed to playing the Service Game before you read this book? The main reason is that you are about to embark on a journey that will take you deep within yourself to explore the very core of who you are as a leader, and it will be uncomfortable at times.

For some of you, this journey will mean unlearning leadership lessons that you should never have learned in the first place. Don't let that prospect discourage you. If you join me on this uncomfortable and yet extremely rewarding journey, you will discover strategies, tools, ideas, and stories that can help you develop the internal resources, mental fortitude, and strength of character needed to grow and excel as an effective, engaging, and transformational leader.

You will be all the better for it. Those around you will thrive because of it. You will obtain a deep sense of joy from it. Our world is desperately in need of it, and this is why.

We are living in exciting and challenging times. Many of the technological and health advances that we see today were mere depictions of science fiction less than a decade ago. It is incredible to witness. And yet, every day, despite all the rapid advances we are making, we are still confronted with a world that is **v**olatile, **u**ncertain, **c**omplex, and **a**mbiguous[2].

Even though we are more productive and live longer than our counterparts less than three generations ago, as leaders, we face stresses of all kinds, and many questions keep us awake at night:

- How do I successfully lead my organisation through a business-critical transformation?

- How do I lead my business to be agile and resilient through globally and economically traumatic events?

- How do I positively engage in matters pertaining to gender prejudice, systemic racism, equity, diversity, and inclusion?

- How do I keep my spouse, customers, shareholders, and my team happy all at the same time?

---

[2] From here on, I will use the abbreviation VUCA to refer to that collection of attributes.

What Game Are You Choosing to Play?

- How do I inspire a remote workforce in a fast-changing digital world?
- How do I stay connected to my kids when I have many other pressing responsibilities?
- How do I contribute to making our world a safer and better place for all?

I have observed the impact that these sorts of pressures and challenges have on many leaders around me, including myself, more of which I'll reveal later in this book. It helped me to come to this realisation:

When life squeezes you and the pressure is on, what you're like on the inside will come out.

This is where the best and most engaging leaders set themselves apart. They have learnt, either intentionally or circumstantially, that if they want to be effective in a way that really matters, they need to be far more consumed with addressing the VUCA within than the VUCA without. And that is no mean feat, which is why many leaders shy away from it. However, our shared journey towards greater levels of personal mastery will positively transform the way you live and lead, enabling you to increase your impact, influence, and resilience.

What Our Journey Will Look Like

This book consists of three parts:

In Part 1 (Chapters 1 and 2), I answer the question, "Why does having a strong core matter?"

- We will take a close look at what our traditional way of leading is costing us – economically, professionally, and personally.
- We will also reconsider what leadership is really about.

In Part 2 (Chapters 3 to 5), I answer the question, "What does it look like to have a strong core?"

- We will discover how we can pursue a much better way of leading and influencing others by tapping into resources deep within us.
- We will define the term **'CORE Leader'** and uncover the four attributes that are foundational in leaders who remain confident, resilient, and effective during the storms of business and life.
- We will also explore how these attributes help you connect with and embrace the heart and currency of leadership.

In Part 3 (Chapters 6 to 10), I answer the question, "How can you develop a strong core?"

- We will unpack strategies for developing internal resilience and strengthening our core.
- We will learn how to walk the walk and not just talk the talk as a transformational leader.

At the end of each chapter, I have included questions for reflection. They are an integral part of our journey. Therefore, I strongly urge you to take the time to answer those questions before moving on.

My Invitation to You

As we get ready to dive in, I'm excited to share parts of Oriah House's poem "The Invitation" with you. It very much resonates with my offer to you to go way deeper and much further than you might be used to as we embark on this journey together.

> It doesn't interest me
> what you do for a living.
> I want to know
> what you ache for
> and if you dare to dream
> of meeting your heart's longing.
>
> It doesn't interest me
> how old you are.
> I want to know
> if you will risk

looking like a fool...
for your dream
for the adventure of being alive...

It doesn't interest me
if the story you are telling me
is true.
I want to know if you can
disappoint another
to be true to yourself.
If you can bear
the accusation of betrayal
and not betray your own soul...

It doesn't interest me
to know where you live
or how much money you have.
It doesn't interest me
who you know
or how you came to be here.
I want to know if you will stand
in the centre of the fire
with me
and not shrink back.

What Game Are You Choosing to Play?

It doesn't interest me
where or what or with whom
you have studied.
I want to know
what sustains you
from the inside
when all else falls away.

I want to know
if you can be alone
with yourself
and if you truly like
the company you keep
in the empty moments.

QUESTIONS FOR REFLECTION

1. As you consider your leadership journey so far, which game have you been playing – the Ego Game or the Service Game?

2. How committed are you to only playing the Service Game? What benefits do you stand to gain?

3. What leadership lessons do you think you may need to unlearn as we journey together?

PART 1

Why Having a Strong Core Matters

"Difficulties break some... but make others."
- NELSON MANDELA

CHAPTER 1

It's Costing Us

*"If you faint in the day of adversity,
how small is your strength!"*
- JEWISH PROVERB

It was just after 6 p.m. on Monday 4 May 2020. The UK was in the middle of its first Covid-19 lockdown, and I was out with my wife, Peju, and our three boys for our 'permitted' daily walk. We have lovely woodlands near us – Tomlinscote Woodlands – which we had walked through many times before, but the lockdown turned it into an adventure and expedition ground for us all.

On this day, as we ambled through, I noticed a fallen tree. What made this so unusual was that every other tree in the area was standing, except for this one. Yes, there had been some heavy winds in previous days, but that didn't explain why this tree, seemingly so tall and robust, was the only one on the ground.

As I took a closer look, the cause became obvious, and I got out my phone to capture the moment.

Now, maybe it was the fact that we were going through a global crisis, it's hard to say, but as I examined the tree and took photos, my first thought was that this was exactly what was happening to so many leaders at that time. You see, the reason this was the only tree on the ground was that it had very shallow roots.

On the outside, many leaders look and sound like they can deliver amidst the storms, demands, and challenges of life and business. They talk results, they talk engagement, they talk productivity, they talk customers, and yet when you dig deeper, something is missing. They haven't got deep internal roots. In other words, many leaders do not have strong and healthy values and principles, nor a firm moral character, that guides them in their leadership and life. That has serious implications.

As I said in the introduction, one of my greatest realisations in recent years is this:

When life squeezes you and the pressure is on, what you're like on the inside will come out.

It doesn't matter how intelligent you are. It doesn't matter what business school you have attended. It doesn't matter how long you have been in a position of leadership. We can pretend all we like to be what we are not. We can try to fake it until we make it. We can put on a façade or pass the blame on to others for our failures, mistakes, or character weaknesses. However, when all is said and done, it is in situations where we face pressures, challenges, and the many curve balls life throws our way as leaders that we reveal who we really are on the inside.

And, if we're brutally honest, many of us have found ourselves in situations where we are barely standing, and our leadership shadow has left a trail of unnecessary damage in its wake.

Let's take an honest look at some of that damage and discover how it impacts all aspects of life.

Financial Health

Do you recognise these values?

- Respect
- Integrity
- Communication
- Excellence

They sound like great values, don't they?
Before the massive accounting fraud scandal that

sent them into bankruptcy in December 2001, those were the corporate values that the Enron Corporation (an energy company based in Houston, Texas, USA) espoused as the guiding principles for how they do what they do.

The problem was that it was all talk. In reality, there was another set of guiding principles driving their leadership culture. In response to a *New York Times* article about the Enron scandal, one person put it like this, "Enron's collapse was a product of the culture of greed, dishonesty, and ethical blindness."

The really sad news about the scandal, which involved the looting of billions of dollars, is that Enron's failure devastated the lives of its 21,000 employees and countless individuals who had invested in the company, as more than $74 billion was lost in the wake of its collapse.

Other high-profile financial scandals, such as the Bernie Madoff Ponzi scheme in the US, which fleeced investors of more than $64 billion, or the $7.4 billion accounting fraud within the South African Retailer, Steinhoff, or the Indian-based global IT firm, Satyam, which falsely boosted earnings by $1.5 billion, are all sobering examples of what happens when those running the show, those with responsibilities to lead, those who many look up to, pay more attention to their external world and their bank balance than to their internal world and character.

These leaders chose to play the Ego Game rather than the Service Game. And so, when the pressure was on – from the market, from shareholders, from competitors, from customers – what they were like on the inside came out, and it wasn't pretty.

When leaders pay more attention to the volatility, uncertainty, complexity, and ambiguity (VUCA) without than the VUCA within, there are sobering financial implications for many. But it doesn't stop there.

Organisational Vitality

According to their 2018 Global Workplace Report, Gallup identifies declining global productivity and human development as one of the world's most serious problems. Across the globe, 85% of employees are not engaged or actively disengaged at work. The economic consequences of this are approximately $7 trillion in lost productivity. The business consequences are poor organisational vitality, low engagement, and suboptimal performance.

The Gallup research goes on to assert that these engagement problems and their resulting consequences within organisations can't be fixed by politics and policies, but only by effective, inspiring, and transformational leaders.

As true as that is, and despite many organisations investing significant amounts in leadership development, it is shocking to see the rising levels of mental health, stress issues, and burnout in the workplace, which continue to have an impact on engagement, on productivity, and on overall organisational health. For example, here in the UK, a Mental Health Foundation study identified that 74% of people have felt so stressed that they have been overwhelmed or unable to cope. One of the primary causes of stress has been work and, sadly, since the 2020 pandemic, this stress has only increased.

I see this reality play out in many organisations – private, public, and voluntary. It comes in many shapes: leaders valuing profit over people, leaders using and mistreating people to get results, leaders driven only to achieve short-term results, leaders high on power and low on service, leaders committed to building their own reputation and then wondering why they're failing to win hearts and minds, or why their people aren't fulfilling their full potential, or why there is so much dysfunction within the organisation.

When leaders pay more attention to their external world, fighting desperately to put out the many fires, navigating the many demands, manoeuvring, politicking, and evading the engagement issues, they leave behind organisations with very little life in them. Organisations with many bodies and very little heart.

As catastrophic as it is, I wish we could say that when leaders play the Ego Game, they only cause damage to shareholder value, organisational vitality, employee engagement, and that it all ends there. But that would be pie in the sky.

The damage isn't just to market value or the life and soul of organisations. It's also personal.

Personal Well-Being

One *Financial Times* article paints a sobering picture about chief executives and senior leaders, when it highlights this, "Chief executives have an above average divorce rate." Why? According to the article, it's because the work never stops, and this has a devastating impact on individuals as well as their families.

The fact that the work never stops is certainly part of the problem, but, in my work with leaders, I see that there is more. It's also because many of these leaders are addicted to controlling things and people around them. They also allow themselves to be influenced more by external factors rather than their own sense of purpose, moral character, values, and mission. As a result, many leaders are almost always mindlessly and literally plugged into the matrix, so to speak, and that comes with consequences.

Some of the leaders I interviewed shared openly and honestly with me about having to confront burnout in their lives. For one, it involved hospitalisation. A few others sought counselling. And some have had to take extended periods of time off to recover.

LEADING FROM YOUR CORE

One interviewee, let's call him Leader X, is a senior leader in a global business. He had a more harrowing story to share with me about the sobering impact of burnout. The situation began as a breakdown in negotiations with a supplier. The negotiation process stalled on a Thursday, and on Friday there was a meeting with the supplier's executive team to try and resolve the issues. Later that evening, one of the key leaders involved, a member of Leader X's team, committed suicide by jumping out of a window. Everyone was shocked. Some felt the business had pushed him to this dark outcome. A few weeks later, more of the story came out. He was having problems at home and was no longer living with his family. He was also having problems at work. He was under a lot of pressure and was struggling to fulfil his responsibilities. Very sadly, it seemed that several factors added to his burnout and overall despair.

This traumatic event was a tough one for Leader X, and many others who were close to this individual, to work through. When Leader X shared some of his learnings with me, two stood out to me: the importance of leaders having healthy release valves to address the pressures they face, and the importance of surfacing our inner conflicts before we reach burnout.

In *The Burnout Society*, the Korean-born German philosopher Byung-Chul Han ends with a haunting observation of most people in the Western world:

"They are too alive to die, and too dead to live." Truly, more leaders need to get in touch with what is happening on the inside before they reach a point of no return.

What are the consequences of not doing this? What are the consequences of not paying attention to our inner world as leaders? Poor marriages. Dysfunctional family relations. Emotionally neglected children. High levels of personal stress. Poor mental health. Dysfunctional work relationships. Depression. Burnout. Sadly, even suicide.

This is real and the cost is personal.

As Duncan Forbes✶ reflected on the leaders he had grown up around, he said this to me,

"I was profoundly affected in my 20s by a senior leader having a nervous breakdown right in front of me... It's very hard for senior leaders who have been brought up on a diet of power and control to connect with their people... It's extraordinary how many leaders I meet who have run away from their humanity."

I cannot tell you how many times I have witnessed this dynamic in leaders. As they take on more and more leadership responsibilities, they slowly forgot what it means to live and thrive as a human being. They forget many of things that matter most in life. They forget to connect with their own heart and mind and soul.

As I observe this, I too am haunted by a question. **As leaders, how in the world can we possibly hope to** win the hearts and minds of those we lead when we cannot even connect with our own?

When leaders, at any level, have power, authority, and influence without a strong and healthy core, they're not only in a position where they can, and so often do, cause damage to an organisation or community and the people around them, but many of them also harm themselves.

These leaders are being rocked to their very core with very little substance to keep them grounded.

The Damage in *My Wake* – Behind Closed Doors

Okay. In case I have given you the impression so far that I have been a mere observer of these phenomena, and the way I have lived and led has always been the perfect expression of what it looks like to have a strong and healthy core where I'm drawing on incredible internal resources, I would like to dispel that notion once and for all, right now.

Despite my genuine desire and passion to connect with and model a more effective, more purposeful, and more transformational way of leading early on in my career, I too have been blinded by all the attraction, allure, and illusion of the Ego Game and have experienced the devastation around me and within.

Almost a decade ago, I went into a period of deep

depression following the failure of yet another business venture. I truly wanted to make a difference with my life via the different ventures I had attempted to set up and failed to get off the ground. I had been trying to control circumstances. I even wanted to control people. I certainly wanted to control the global market. But none of that was meant to be. At one point, I was paying our mortgage on the credit card for several months. The failure and the financial pressure put a heavy strain on my marriage, family life, and personal well-being.

Years later, my career recovered, my debts were paid off, and I was travelling the world as a consultant for an award-winning culture change and employee engagement agency, working with great clients, transforming organisations, developing leaders, redefining, and shaping how organisations engaged their people. Several promotions later, I was on the Board of our agency, influencing business strategy, working with senior clients, and feeling good about the future, and yet, closer to home… No, in fact, I mean, at home and within myself, things weren't what they needed to be. I wasn't exactly walking my talk.

Despite the growing success, I continued to be plagued with doubt, anxiety, fear, internal conflict, and impostor syndrome. What's more, Peju felt I was distant. Present in body, but not in heart and mind. I wasn't fully engaging with our three young and exuberant boys either. I guess you could say that I had 'outsourced' a lot of the connecting and parenting to her. Truth is, I was enjoying riding the wave of career success. I figured that all I needed was some time to invest in building a solid and robust career, and then I could give Peju and our boys all the attention they needed.

I will never forget one conversation Peju and I had when she said something along the lines of, "I'm afraid that as you pursue all your dreams and achieve them, you'll get to a point where you have it all – all the success and all the kudos and all the recognition – but when you look back at me and the boys, we're not here."

That was a hard message to accept.

It has been said that the longest distance in the world is the 12-18 inches between our heads and our hearts. I would love to say that Peju's words resonated so deeply with me that I immediately had a change of heart and turned things around. Alas, that is not how the story played out, at least not for a few years.

That said, I did begin a journey of reconnecting with many of the values and ideals that I hold true and, as I did, I came to a deeper understanding of the truth of these words from an early mediaeval text:

"The hardest victory is over self."

I can tell you from deep, real, and personal experience how true that is. **It's so much easier to play the Ego**

It's Costing Us

Game. It's so much easier to tell people what to do. It's so much easier to create an environment of dependency rather than empowerment. It's so much easier to govern through compliance rather than inspire greater levels of passion and ownership in others. It's so much easier to talk the talk than walk the walk as a leader. It's so much easier to focus on controlling our external circumstances. It's so much easier to expect others to change and not change ourselves. It's so much easier to focus on what's in our self-interest rather than on what truly serves others. And yet… and yet… we confine ourselves to the Ego Game to the peril of organisations, to the peril of the economy, to the peril of those we lead, to the peril of the communities that we're part of, to the peril of our loved ones, and even to the peril of ourselves.

Playing the Ego Game as leaders, unfortunately, means paying more attention to what is happening on the outside than to what is happening on the inside. And it comes at a price. That price is the financial health of organisations. That price is the vibrancy and motivation and passion of the people and teams we lead. That price is our personal well-being.

If we continue down that path, when we all get to the end of our careers and lives and look back, I can't imagine that anyone of us would be convinced it was a price worth paying.

There is a much better way for us to live and lead, but it means unlearning some old lessons, relearning new ones, and going deeper than we may have ever willingly gone before.

It will require doing the hard work of developing a greater level of mental fortitude, emotional intelligence, and moral character strength than is typical for many leaders.

Are you ready?

QUESTIONS FOR REFLECTION

1. How would you describe the impact of your leadership style on those around you?

2. Catholic monk Thomas Merton once said, "People may spend their whole lives climbing the ladder of success only to find, once they reach the top, that the ladder is leaning against the wrong wall." How confident are you that the ladder you are climbing is leaning against the right wall?

3. What price are you currently paying for the way you live and lead? Is that price worth it?

CHAPTER 2

What You Really Think About Leadership Matters

"Leadership is never given on a silver platter, one has to earn it."
- ELLEN JOHNSON SIRLEAF

As we continue this journey of discovering what it means and looks like to live and lead with a strong and healthy core, we need to take a brief but necessary detour. The question of what leadership means is an essential one to settle in your mind, and perhaps even reframe, before we go any further.

Three of the most meaningful definitions of leadership I've come across over the years are:

"Leadership is the skill of influencing people to work enthusiastically towards goals identified as being for the common good." – James C. Hunter, The Servant

"Leadership is courageous, authentic influence that creates enduring value." – Kevin Cashman, Leadership from the Inside Out

"Leadership is positive influence." – John C. Maxwell, The 21 Irrefutable Laws of Leadership

I heard an incredible array of responses to that question from all the leaders I interviewed for this book. I'd like to share a selection of those with you. However, before you read on, I suggest you first reflect on and capture your own answer to this question...

What does leadership mean to you?

This is what leadership means to me, and this is how I think about leadership:

_____
_____
_____
_____
_____
_____
_____
_____
_____
_____

Done?
Great. Now, you can read on.

Leadership/A leader is…

"Someone who is not afraid to grow the people around them." - THIRUSELVAAM MATEEN

"Demonstrating more curiosity and more guts than others, and the capability and motivation to galvanise people to fight for a worthwhile purpose." - AMADOU DIALLO

"Creating an environment that stimulates exceptional performance." - AVRON EPSTEIN

"Showing the way and walking with people to get to the stated goal." - DAMON HART

"The ability to be others-centred and understand that there's a greater force that you must submit to and serve." - FEMI OMERE

"Being of service to the wider whole and being prepared to make tough decisions." - HELEN CRESSWELL

"Inspiring people to achieve a goal, removing barriers, solving problems, and building trust." - JESS MULLINGER

"Using your skills as a force for good, with a humble approach." - KATARZYNA MARCZEWSKA

"Authenticity, humility and not being afraid to make the difficult decisions." - LINDSAY BRIDGES

"Somebody that has a bigger picture, sees three or four steps ahead of most people, sees both the trees and the forest and understands what is necessary for the trees to grow, individually and collectively." - MELISSA RIBEIRO

"Influencing people to see a vision, catch a vision, and follow a vision." - OMMO CLARK

"Recognising that you win with others and never alone." - YVES TOURNIER

"Helping others to see the greatness in themselves." - DAVID BANG

Those are some incredible definitions of leadership, and I could share many more.

Personally, **I like to define leadership as relating to others in a way that unleashes the best of their motivation, passion, creativity, and energy towards a worthwhile goal.**

But why does any of that matter? Why does it matter how you define leadership or what you think about it?

What You Really Think About Leadership Matters

When I was 18, a mentor of mine gave me a copy of Stephen Covey's book *The 7 Habits of Highly Effective People*, and I loved it! I probably scribbled notes on every page. There were so many ideas that blew me away. One, in particular, is relevant to the questions above. It is this: "Private victory precedes public victory."

Sadly, many leaders are all about the public victory. Niki Frank* probably nailed it when he said, "The reason so many leaders don't value personal mastery skills is because they can get results without it – in the short term. Unfortunately, they're not aware of the long-lasting impact of poor personal mastery skills."

As leaders, the long-lasting victory that we desire to have with our people, with our teams, and in our organisations is only possible when it's based on the personal, private victory of knowing what we stand for, having strong moral character, staying true to our values, and connecting with our own sense of purpose.

You see, the reason many leaders do not have deep internal roots is that they haven't done the hard work of pursing the private victory in four key areas:

1. **Values** – They haven't done the hard work of developing clear, compelling, and congruent values, grounding themselves in what they stand for as a person and as a leader.

2. **Worldview or Mindset** – They haven't done the hard work of developing a worldview that guides

their decisions and choices and helps them and those around them to thrive, even in tough times.

3. **Habits** – They haven't done the hard work of cultivating mental, behavioural, and attitudinal habits that maximise their energy, positivity, and contribution to the world.

4. **Beliefs** – They haven't done the hard work of surfacing and overcoming their limiting beliefs and nurturing those beliefs that empower themselves and others instead of beliefs that hinder or sabotage their effectiveness and fulfilment as a leader and as a person.

Without this private victory, you will never have the resilience needed to navigate the challenges that leading others will throw your way. Without this, you'll find that you are running on empty far too often. Without this, you just won't have the positive impact that you desire to have.

And so, the reason it matters what you think about leadership is that if leadership is primarily about authority to you, if leadership is something you feel you deserve because of your achievements, if leadership is essentially a title, then I can guarantee that you will never win the hearts and minds of those you lead. Instead, leadership will always be an uphill struggle that is about the rewards you get and never really about the long-lasting difference you make.

What You Really Think About Leadership Matters

The reason it matters how you define leadership is that if you truly believe that leading others is about influencing and inspiring them to be their best selves and harnessing the best of their motivation, passion, creativity, and energy towards a common goal that makes a positive difference in our world, then you will know that the only way to do that effectively and authentically is by becoming the best version of you.

After all, when life inevitably squeezes you as a leader, when the pressure is on, what you truly believe about leadership and what you truly believe about others will come out.

As a leader, you cannot give what you don't have.

Leadership vs Management

There's one more idea we need to address as we consider what leadership means to us.

I'll start by sharing with you the number one complaint I have heard from many leaders over the years: "I wish I didn't have to deal with all these people issues, so I could just get on with my day job."

Surprise, surprise, as a leader, dealing with 'people' issues, engaging with people, connecting with people, partnering with people, inspiring people, creating psychological safety for people is all part of the day job. But, of course, it depends on how you see leadership.

If you look back to the definitions of leadership that I shared above, you'll notice that not one person referred to the term 'manager'. Over the years, I've come to the conviction that 'manager' in relation to people is a very poor term and suggests a faulty paradigm about leading and inspiring others.

In their book, *Rare Leadership,* Marcus Warner and Jim Wilder write this, "Management is the efficient accomplishment of tasks. Leadership is producing and maintaining full engagement from our group in what matters."

James C. Hunter pointed out in his book *The Servant*, "Management is something we do with things. We manage our finances, we manage inventory, we manage our resources. We do not manage people."

If you want to be an effective and transformational leader, this is a critical mindset to have – you manage things and lead people.

And this is not just semantics. You only have to observe someone transitioning from being an individual contributor – managing tasks and interacting with others – to being a team leader or supervisor to see that this is way more fundamental. Initially, many first-line (and first-time) supervisors and leaders approach the people they now lead in the same way as the tasks they were used to managing.

What You Really Think About Leadership Matters

Sadly, many leaders continue this approach even into senior leadership positions. People are just numbers that need to be managed, controlled, or used.

If you really want to lead effectively, purposefully, and courageously, then you must understand that because people have a mind, because people have innate creativity, because people are full of untapped potential, because people have a heart and soul, they need leading and not managing.

With that important detour addressed, let's recap our journey so far.

We have established that the traditional and typical ways of leading – from a place of authority, from a place of superiority, by virtue of our position, by focusing primarily on the VUCA without, with the perspective of people as things to be managed and not people to be inspired – is costing us dearly. It's costing us the financial health of our businesses. It's costing us the vibrant vitality of our organisations and communities. It's costing us thriving families and marriages. It's costing us our health.

There is a much better way, and it begins by looking in a direction that is alien to most.

QUESTIONS FOR REFLECTION

1. How do you define leadership?

2. In what ways do you need to reframe what leadership means to you?

3. Would others describe you more as a leader or as a manager?

PART 2

What a Strong Core Looks Like

"Men and women of genius are admired, men and women of wealth are envied, men and women of power are feared; but only men and women of character are trusted."

- ALFRED ADLER

CHAPTER 3

The Audacity to Focus Within

"There is nothing noble in being superior to your fellow man; true nobility is being superior to your former self."
- UNKNOWN AUTHOR

Our journey together has reached a critical point. Said in a hundred different ways, the main point so far is that the best leaders, the most effective leaders, the most resilient leaders pay more attention to the VUCA within than the VUCA without. They pay more attention to mastering self than mastering others. They pay more attention to inner conflicts than outer conflicts.

In *The Power of Now*, Eckhart Tolle says, "Be at least as interested in what goes on inside you as what happens outside. If you get the inside right, the outside will fall into place." I hope that even if you still have some reservations about what this means practically, given our journey so far, the truth and wisdom in those words are beginning to resonate deep within you.

However, at this stage of our journey, even if you are convinced that it is important to pay more attention to what is happening on the inside, it wouldn't surprise me if you are wondering, "But, Obi, what exactly does that look like?" "Are you suggesting I take time away from work, go to a Buddhist temple, and practice meditation?" While that is not an outrageous idea, I agree that it is time for me to clearly answer a few questions:

- What does it look like to pay more attention to what is happening on the inside?
- How does that lead to a strong core?
- And what difference will it really make to your life and leadership?

I will answer those questions. Let me begin by showing you what it takes to start looking in a different direction to most leaders.

A Change of Direction

One of the people I interviewed for this book, who is also a mentor of mine, is Stephen Howard✶. Stephen has been at the helm of many organisations and knows what it's like to face the day-to-day pressures of addressing evolving customer needs, changing employee needs, harnessing the motivation and creativity of employees, business growth challenges, competitor challenges, the need to innovate and remain relevant in the marketplace, and so on.

When I asked what helped him to develop the resilience of character and mind to successfully navigate these challenges as a senior leader, Stephen said that, early on in his career, managing the pressures of leadership wasn't something he always did well, but there was a moment when things changed.

It was his first international assignment, and he'd been tasked with opening a ceramics factory in Calcutta, India. On one trip, shortly after he boarded a local flight leaving for Calcutta, he noticed a little lady board the plane too. She was wearing a simple white sari with three blue stripes on the border. It was a recognisable outfit. One that many people around the world had come to associate with this lady.

There were only two seats left on the plane, and it just so happened that one of those seats was next to Stephen. His gaze was fixed on her as she walked down the aisle. A few moments later, Mother Teresa was strapping herself into the seat next to him.

They exchanged pleasantries and Stephen heard her say, "What do you do?" As he proceeded to answer the question, including preparing to share a little about his current assignment, she touched his leg and said, "No.

What do you do that matters? What are you going to do with your life that really matters?"

As Stephen tells the story, the rest of the conversation is a bit of a blur because the questions hit him like a ton of bricks. Those are the sort of questions that result in a change of direction – from paying more attention to all the things that you're doing and achieving (external focus), along with all the demands and challenges that come with it, to paying attention to your sense of purpose (internal focus) and all the things that truly resonate with your own heart and mind.

Now, we can't all have conversations with the likes of Mother Teresa, but we can ask ourselves questions about what really matters in our lives and begin to connect, or reconnect, with our own hearts and minds as we turn the focus within and increase our level of self-awareness.

For John Heard✶, self-awareness is where it all begins as a leader: "If I'm leading people, I need to know people, and that means I need to know myself."

Going Deeper

In Chapter 2, I said that far too many leaders look and sound like they are resilient, but when you dig deeper, and when the storms and challenges of business and life and ethics come their way, you find that they are far too easily uprooted because they have very shallow roots. They don't have the internal structure that is characteristic of someone with a strong and healthy core.

Now, it's time to define exactly what I mean by having a strong and healthy core. I'm specifically referring to these attributes:

C – Clear Values
O – Optimistic Worldview
R – Rewarding Habits
E – Empowering Beliefs

From here on, as we continue our journey, I'll use the term **'CORE Leader'** to refer to a resilient, engaging, and transformational leader who has integrated these attributes into their life, enabling them to lead with purpose, authenticity, and courage. As we will see on our journey, these attributes also help CORE Leaders to maximise their energy and increase their impact.

Let's take a look at these four attributes in a bit more detail.

C = Clear Values

Have you ever asked yourself: Who am I? Why am I here? What am I about? Why do I do the work that I do? What matters most to me? What gets me out of bed in the morning?

CORE Leaders are the people who have put in the work to develop congruent and compelling answers to those questions. And by congruent and compelling, I mean that the answers are so clear that they resonate deep within their soul.

But why? Why is it so critical that you are clear about your values if you want to maximise your energy, increase your impact, and build resilience as a leader?

There are three main reasons. Having clear values helps you:

1. Course Correct

Just like a plane that has gone off target and needs to course correct, your values help you know what you stand for and get back on track when you are slightly or significantly off target. We all make mistakes and lose ourselves sometimes, but when you are clear about your values, you can realign yourself to what matters most. "It's important to have a clear set of values that serve as a compass and give you the ability to make the right choices," that is how Mathias Lingnau✱ put it to me. For Charles Sekwalor✱, this is absolutely essential for all leaders. As he told me, "We have to deal with a lot of noise as leaders in the form of all sorts of demands and pressures. The only way to deal with the noise is to have a clear sense of purpose that anchors you. When you know what you're about and what matters most to you, you remain grounded." Knowing your values helps you reconnect with the coordinates of your life and clarify the impact that you want to have.

2. Stay Anchored

One leader I interviewed told me about a challenging merger she was part of. She was pressured into making some unethical decisions just to make the numbers look good. For her, that was the straw that broke the camel's back. Her values were compromised, and she knew that that wasn't an environment she wanted to be in anymore. For every leader, there will be moments of truth, there will be times when people expect you to do something that isn't in line with your values. "Things easily go wrong at home and work when you don't have strong values, but knowing your values helps you make the right trade-offs," says Kim MacGillavry✶. Andrew Agerbak✶ agrees. With regards to the importance of our values, he said, "I've had opportunities presented to me where I would have earned double what I'm on but would have had to compromise my personal values and priorities. That wasn't something I was prepared to do."

Another leader who also had to confront unethical decisions and practices in her business said, "It takes courage to speak out when something is not right or when something goes against your principles. It takes courage to get your ego out of the way and focus on what is right. When you have clarity about who you are, it is so much easier." If you are uncertain about your values, you won't be able to stand up for what is right, for others, or for yourself. You will be tossed and turned by every external wave, never really taking full responsibility for your life and attitude because you don't really know what you stand for.

3. Leave a Legacy that Counts

At a time when many leaders were more interested in setting up monuments in their name, the influential Greek statesman and orator, Pericles, who lived between 495 and 429 BC, was someone who had a strong handle on the true test of one's impact as a leader. Here's what he said, "What you leave behind is not what is engraved in stone monuments, but what is woven into the lives of others." That sort of understanding about the impact of our legacy only comes when we have uncovered our deepest values and live them out every day through our choices and decisions. It helps us live with a greater sense of purpose about what really matters at home and in the workplace. Emma Sexton✷ told me that she often asks herself, "Where is my decision-making coming from, ego or purpose and values?" That's a great question for all of us to ask as leaders when we consider the legacy that we want to leave behind. It has been said, "Today's footprint is tomorrow's legacy." **If you are not clear about what you stand for, if your values conflict with how you live and operate as a leader, then do not be surprised by the impoverished legacy you will leave behind.**

The Audacity to Focus Within

CORE Leaders have clear values. They are deeply and consciously aware of what is most important, to themselves and others, which enables them to lead with a greater sense of authenticity. Having clear, compelling, and congruent values allows them to make better decisions that are aligned to their true north. They live with and on purpose.

O = Optimistic Worldview

What would you say if I told you that…

… we are living in the most peaceful time ever in human history?

… we have a fraction of the level of violence that existed over 500 years ago?

… over the last 100 years, the per capita income (adjusted for inflation) for every person on the planet has more than tripled?

… every nation on earth has gotten healthier and wealthier?

… the human lifespan has more than doubled?

… the cost of food has come down 13-fold? The cost of energy 20-fold? The cost of transportation 100-fold? The cost of communication 1000-fold?

I know, I know, you're probably thinking, "Obi, what news do you pay attention to?" And, you know what, that is a great question. When you look at the news today, most of what you hear is all the bad stuff going on – the wars, the deaths, the poverty, the crime, the hostile takeovers. And yet, as I alluded to earlier in this book, all over the world we have access to technology today that our grandparents could only dream of. For me, this reinforces the reality that we all live in one of two worlds – a world where the glass is half empty or one where the glass is half full.

In his book *Good to Great*, Jim Collins describes a leader who was an incredible example of someone with an optimistic worldview in the most difficult of circumstances. Admiral James Stockdale, who was a prisoner of war (POW) during the Vietnam War, describes what it was like in the POW camp and which of his fellow prisoners survived. He told Jim Collins that there were three groups of prisoners. There were the ones who said, "We're going to be out tomorrow. If not tomorrow, then next week. And if not then, the week after." They were the ones who had an unrealistic view of what it would take to release them. Those prisoners did not survive. There was a second group of prisoners who said things like, "We're done! We're finished! We're not getting out!" They didn't make it either. The prisoners who survived were the ones with a firm sense of reality uniquely fused with optimism, "We don't know when we're going to get out, but we're convinced that we will make it."

This story illustrates my favourite description of optimism:

The Audacity to Focus Within

"Optimism is accepting reality while still believing that the best is yet to come."

I also love the way Shirzad Chamine, author of *Positive Intelligence*, describes optimism as the 'Sage Perspective', which is about recognising that every outcome or circumstance can be turned into a gift and opportunity.

An optimistic worldview is a powerful and energising way of viewing the world. Not having an optimistic worldview causes us to self-sabotage and stop just when we are at the finish line. Not having an optimistic worldview prevents us from the seeing the incredible potential in others. Not having an optimistic worldview causes us to see obstacles as evidence that we are on the wrong path. On the other hand, having an optimistic worldview makes a difference in three key areas.

It helps you:

1. Build Mental Fitness and Resilience

Mental fitness is often defined as your capacity to respond to life's challenges with a positive rather than a negative mindset. You're more likely to push through and go the extra mile when you have the mindset that, despite what is going on around you, the best is yet to come, and that there is a gift or opportunity in your current circumstance, no matter what it is. Recently, I was working with some leaders in the aviation industry as they sought to rebuild their business following the devastation caused by the global pandemic. Some of the leaders described how this mindset helped them create opportunities, in the middle of the pandemic, that they had never considered beforehand simply because they believed there was good that could come out of even the most challenging of circumstances.

2. Increase Your Chances of Success

Shawn Achor, author of *The Happiness Advantage*, has done an incredible amount of research into the power of optimism. According to him, "Success does not equate to happiness, but greater levels of optimism, happiness, and positivity absolutely lead to greater levels of success." When you have an optimistic worldview, you end up doing more, dreaming more, believing more, and achieving more than you thought possible. Leaders with an optimistic worldview inspire others to keep going when the rest of the world would have given up.

3. Positively Influence Others

When you believe, despite all the challenges you are facing, that you can get through it, you inspire others to take action. Who would the people you lead rather work with – someone who accepts reality while still believing the best is yet to come, or someone who only sees the challenges? I know what my answer is. As Christoph Bäumer✶ said, "It's the sort of mindset that helps leaders be calm and patient when all others are getting nervous and confused."

As a leader, your outlook on life and the meaning you give to the different events you face shape your everyday decisions, as well as the quality of your interactions with the people around you.

A CORE Leader is someone with an optimistic outlook, grounded in reality. That worldview motivates them to lead more courageously and influence those around them to dream more, achieve more, and become more than they ever imagined.

R = Rewarding Habits

Every day, we make decisions and choices about what we are going to do, how we are going to show up as leaders, what difference we want to make. We like to think those choices and decisions are well thought out and considered daily, but the reality is that they are not. They are based on habits – those automatic sequences of actions that we engage in every day. Habits are powerful and constantly influence our attitude and energy.

Among many who have written on the topic of habit formation, the American Pulitzer prize-winning reporter and bestselling author of *The Power of Habit*, Charles Duhigg, has made a great contribution to the world of personal growth and development by shedding tremendous light on why habits exist, how they can be changed, and what power they have over our personal lives and in the workplace.

In his book, he shares this insight: "Habits aren't destiny... habits can be ignored, changed, or replaced. But... When a habit emerges, the brain stops fully participating in decision making. It stops working so hard, or diverts focus to other tasks. So, unless you deliberately fight a habit – unless you find new routines – the pattern will unfold automatically."

The good news is that habits don't have to control us forever. They can be changed. The tough news is that **changing our habits requires intention**, as our old habits will not give up without a fight, especially because so many of these habits are mental, emotional, and attitudinal.

This is where CORE Leaders set themselves apart. They are intentionally focused on cultivating rewarding habits – habits that maximise their energy, their resilience, their attitude, their courage, and their impact every day. These rewarding mental, behavioural, and attitudinal habits are powerful levers for transforming the way they lead.

It may be true that our habits aren't our destiny, but it has also been said, "We first make our habits, then our habits make us." Our emotional, social, physical, mental, and spiritual habits *do* make us because they shape our character. More on that in Chapter 5.

E = Empowering Beliefs

Why do your beliefs matter?

According to the dictionary, a belief is any thought or idea that someone accepts as true. It is an acceptance that something exists.

What should strike you most here is that a belief or opinion doesn't have to *be* true, it just has to be *accepted* as true by the person who holds that belief or opinion.

So, does it matter if a belief is true or not?

Well, just consider the many atrocities that have been committed over the course of history because of what people *believed* to be true. Think about the crusades, the slave trade, the holocaust, the 9/11 bombings, or systemic racism. These things occurred and exist because of what specific individuals or groups of individuals *believed* or *believe* to be true.

At the same time, many amazing feats have been accomplished because of what people *believed* to be true. Just think about the work of the Wright brothers, who believed it was possible to create a contraption that would enable human beings to fly – and today we have the airline industry. Can you imagine what international travel would be like without it? Or consider Roger Bannister, who believed it was possible to break the four-minute mile barrier. Since he achieved the impossible on 6 May 1954, hordes of others have gone on to break it too because they now believe it is possible.

Clearly, **beliefs can work for us and against us.**

Bruce Lipton, author of *The Biology of Belief*, says, "Our beliefs control our bodies, our minds, and our lives. In a sense, beliefs are the software of leadership. Our deeply personal operating system that runs the show on the surface."

As a leader, your beliefs matter because they create your consciousness, which creates your habits, actions, and behaviours, which, ultimately, determine your results. If you want to lead with purpose, authenticity, and courage, then you need to examine your beliefs. If you want to be a resilient, engaging, and transformational leader, then you need to examine your beliefs. If you're not happy with the results you are getting or the impact you are having, then you need to examine your beliefs.

Where do our beliefs come from? For many of us, the beliefs we have today were shaped and informed by our environment and the authority figures we grew up around.

This is the typical evolution of the belief system we each have today:

- Firstly, parents, teachers, coaches, religious leaders, friends, relatives, and other people of influence in a child's life say to the child: "This is fact." "This is true." "This is what the world is like." "This is what you must be like."

- Next, in general, the child accepts the perception

and beliefs of these influential figures as fact – even if those perceptions and beliefs are completely wrong.
- Then, the child unconsciously internalises the beliefs in their subconscious and builds habits and values accordingly.
- Finally, the child grows into an adult, going about life with dozens and dozens of faulty beliefs and habits, unfortunately without being consciously aware of it.

Many of us walk around with beliefs – about ourselves, about others, about the world, about leadership – that are limiting and unhelpful, and yet we do not question them because we have lived with them for so long. We set invisible boundaries for our lives with a corrupted narrative and faulty internal operating system driving the show. It's no wonder self-talk expert Shad Helmstetter says, "We are most comfortable with the thoughts we have lived with the most. It makes no difference if those thoughts aren't the best for us – it's what we know, it's what we are most secure in keeping at our side."

Not all our beliefs about life, about people, about business, about leadership are helpful. **As leaders, it is essential that we intentionally examine our beliefs so that they empower us and those around us.** After all, what you believe about leadership, what you believe about yourself, what you believe about others, and what you believe about life impacts your contribution, your legacy, your effectiveness, and your influence on others as a leader.

CORE Leaders understand this and do the hard work of overcoming self-defeating behaviours by becoming more aware of their destructive and limiting beliefs, and intentionally nurturing empowering ones. In Part 3, we will look at how they do this.

Keeping the Focus Within

You have now started to get a clearer picture of what it looks like to have a strong and healthy core. **A CORE Leader has clear values, an optimistic worldview, rewarding habits, and empowering beliefs.** These are the foundations of a strong internal structure and healthy core. These are the foundations of the high levels of self-awareness required to lead with courage and impact and purpose.

As Melonae Thomas✶ said to me, "It's impossible to be a good leader if you don't have a good sense of self-awareness. Without that you'll never know the imprint you're leaving on others." And Teresa Hickman✶ added, "If you don't change the core, no amount of external resources will help. You have to be willing to dig deep!"

And we will certainly go deeper in Part 3, as we look at how to strengthen our core in all four areas.

The Audacity to Focus Within

Before then, it is important to know that having a strong and healthy core not only helps you become a more resilient, self-aware, and engaging leader, but that it is also the gateway to connecting with and embracing the heart and currency of leadership.

It's time to turn our attention to these, beginning with the heart of leadership.

QUESTIONS FOR REFLECTION

1. How important has personal mastery been to you so far?

2. Do you know what you stand for?

3. Do you have a worldview that guides your decisions and helps you and those around you to thrive, even in tough times?

4. Have you cultivated mental and behavioural habits to maximise your energy, positivity, and contribution to the world?

5. What life events and experiences have most shaped your belief system?

6. Do your main beliefs propel you forward and empower those around you, or do they hinder your impact in leadership and in life?

CHAPTER 4

The Heart of Leadership

"Serving others breaks you free from the shackles of self and self-absorption that choke out the joy of living."
- JAMES C. HUNTER

It can be tempting to think that the answer to the 'management vs leadership' debate, described in Chapter 2, is to simply get rid of the term 'manager' and call everyone who has the responsibility to lead others a 'leader'.

This is where I need to be crystal clear that our journey together is not merely about terminology, but about being. It's about who you are, who you are becoming, and whether you really get what leadership is about.

The Heart of It All

In my work with leaders around the world, those leaders who stifle and limit the potential of their teams, organisations, or communities, directly and indirectly, are the ones who think it's all about them. They won't admit it, but when you observe the way they lead and use their power and influence, it's more for their own benefit than for the good of others. They might have good intentions to look after their people, but they still lead in a way that ultimately breeds helplessness, dependency, or compliance.

They have missed the true heart of it all, and it shows up in their fundamental beliefs about people, about power, about governance, and about control.

Nikki Craig✶ describes it this way, "'My way or the highway' type of leadership stifles organisations. Instead, our position of power and strength should be used to create a common vision and purpose, bringing people together." Joe Mamone✶ seems to agree when he says, "Leadership isn't about authority. It's about being in service of other people. It's getting people to follow not because of your title, but because they're confident in the direction you're going, and they know that you're committed to helping them be the best they can."

A few years ago, I participated in a three-day leadership conference in Lubbock, Texas. The conference was attended by CEOs and their senior leadership teams, and it covered topics such as building a purpose-driven business, aligning culture around a clear set of values, leadership styles, and the like. As I read the bios of the various speakers, I noticed that one of the breakout speakers described himself and his wife as the 'stewards' of their family-run company. Not CEO. Not founder. Steward.

I was immediately drawn to that description and ended up having a great conversation with the speaker later that day. He described how this was more than a title. It was a way of leading, seeing people, and using power that was visible in their HR policies for hiring, remuneration, engaging people, and so on. I couldn't help but wonder, what would happen if more leaders – from front-line supervisors to CEOs – saw themselves first and foremost as stewards, responsible for doing their absolute best to govern, grow, and nurture someone else's assets, even if it was a business that they had founded or co-founded?

In *Firms of Endearment*, Raj Sisodia, David Wolfe, and Jag Sheth describe the impact of this kind of leadership in creating organisations (known as FoEs) that "endear themselves to stakeholders by bringing the interests of all stakeholder groups (society, partners, investors, customers, and employees) into strategic alignment." This means that every group of stakeholders only benefits when other groups do too. Companies with this culture meet the functional and psychological needs of their stakeholders in a refreshing way that engenders an incredible fondness for the company.

The business results of such companies are extraordinary. According to the research, these FoEs returned 1,180.17% for investors over a 15-year period, compared to 262.91% from those companies cited in *Good to Great*. What at an incredible endorsement!

Leaders in these companies also demonstrate living with an optimistic worldview. According to Sisodia et al., "Instead of seeing the world in narrow, constricted terms, they see its infinite positive possibilities. They believe deeply in the possibility of a rising tide that raises all boats. Faced with competitive threat, they don't look to cut prices and costs and employees, but to add greater value."

Someone else who has done a lot to champion and highlight the overwhelmingly positive impact of stewardship is Peter Block.

In *Stewardship: Choosing Service over Self-Interest*, Block defines stewardship as "accountability without control or compliance." Leaders who consider themselves stewards give people in the organisation more choices and freedom. **Rather than controlling people, it is a matter of taking accountability for the well-being of the organisation by being of service to others.**

As a CORE Leader, the more power you can distribute courageously and wisely, the more people you can serve across your organisation. This is truly the heart of leadership.

In no way is stewardship about abdication. Rather, it is built on some fundamental beliefs:

1. People do their best work when they connect with a purpose that transcends short-term interests.
2. Empowerment and ownership are at the heart of driving and sustaining innovation, vitality, and growth in any enterprise.
3. The more control and autonomy people have over their own work, the greater the creativity and motivation they bring to it.
4. As leaders, our power should be used on behalf of others and not for ourselves.

The Business Case for Stewardship

None of this is new, but the overwhelming pull of the Ego Game stops many leaders from seeing the incredible value of living and leading this way. Stewardship as a way of leading is a scary prospect for many leaders. What do you do if the power and authority you have isn't all about protecting your empire, your reputation, or your compensation package?

In *Stewardship*, Block goes on to highlight the business case for driving a culture of service over self-interest in our organisations and communities:

- Stewardship enables a system of governance that is most likely to give the person who has most contact with the customer or other key stakeholders the resources, knowledge, and mindset to give the right response
- Stewardship drives greater innovation and growth because our people feel greater levels of ownership, passion, and commitment for the cause
- Stewardship leads to organisations adapting more quickly to customers and stakeholders
- Stewardship leads to greater control of costs and shorter product- or service-creation cycle times

This is truly a no-brainer and the pay-off in terms of engagement and impact is huge. Think about it. How many of us have been impressed by the customer experience representative who is clearly empowered to address our concerns and recover a situation compared to the customer experience representative who hides behind company policy for fear of blame?

Many leaders complain about all the challenges and troubles that keep them awake at night as they lead their businesses, and yet, as we consider the power of stewardship as a way of leading, it's worth asking, what impact would this way of leading have on the stress levels of leaders and the engagement of our people?

The answer is that many leaders would sleep more soundly, and many of their people would feel free to make a greater difference and impact as they tap into more of their motivation, energy, and passion.

Getting Your Heart Back

So, how do you begin to integrate stewardship in the way you lead? How do you get your heart back as a leader?

For starters, the following three actions will help.

1. Confront Your Desire for Dominance and Control

Most, if not all, leaders have targets and results they're aiming for. The desire to achieve those results often becomes so all-consuming that many leaders feel compelled to do whatever it takes, which often means controlling the uncontrollable – people. They assert their authority. They compromise on their values. They micro-manage. They use their power and influence to create an environment of dependency and compliance. They think it's easier that way. They think it means they can guarantee the outcomes that they want. However, while this may achieve compliance and control, it will never unleash the discretionary effort of people who have found their passion for a cause bigger than themselves. Focusing on empowerment and service, instead of dominance and control helps your people tap into a purpose that transcends all short-term interests.

2. Stay Close to Where the Action Is

Part of the challenge of leadership is that the typical hierarchy in most organisations means that as you develop as a leader, you move further away from the frontline action and often lose touch with the reality of the day-to-day challenges your people, stakeholders, or customers actually face. To counter that, depending on your environment as a leader, make it a habit to regularly connect with and understand the worlds of those you influence – talk directly to your customers, walk the floor of your business, have lunch with frontline colleagues, speak to people in your community. Don't just analyse organisational data, get under the skin of it by having real conversations with the people at the coalface of your organisation. Also, if you see your role as removing obstacles for your people or solving your customers' challenges, the only way you can truly do that is to intimately understand the obstacles and challenges as best as you can.

3. Guard Yourself against the Danger of Privileges and Abuse of Power

I absolutely believe in leaders being rewarded for their work, contribution, and results. However, the privileges you receive by virtue of your position can easily go to your head and cause you to rely on your power, authority, position, and intelligence to influence others, instead of your character and your commitment to service. That's when leaders begin to abuse their position, make unethical decisions, and compromise their values. That's also when they begin to lose the respect of those who look up to them. So put checks in place to guard against abusing your position and the privileges that come with it.

Our world needs leaders who are more devoted to serving others than themselves. More devoted to using their power for the good of others than protecting their rewards and reputation. The payoff is not only improved performance, results, and engagement in our organisations, but also a sound night's sleep for many leaders.

Invest in Building the Capacity of the Next Generation of Leaders

When you consider that the idea of stewardship is often linked to managing the estate of another until their heir is ready to assume responsibility for it, you can't help but picture how much better our world would be if all leaders adopted this mindset and were committed to leaving their community, organisation, or country better for the next generation than they found it.

Sometime in June 2020, still in the middle of the Covid-19 pandemic, I was having a conversation with a senior leader of a voluntary organisation. We were discussing the vision of the organisation, and like so many organisations and businesses at that time, it was navigating the fallout of the pandemic and all the uncertainty that went with it.

I have a lot of respect for this leader and, as he talked about his vision for the organisation, I was reminded why. One of the things he said was, "When it comes to where we're going and what our vision is, I like to look not only five or ten years ahead, but to think about what it could be like in 50 or 100 years..."

Now, you might be thinking, "So what, Obi? He thinks of the big picture. Great. A lot of leaders do that. What makes that so engaging and transformational?"

Well, it's what he said afterwards that really revealed how connected he was to the true heart of leadership.

Here's what he said in full, "When it comes to where we're going and what our vision is, I like to look not only five or ten years ahead, but to think about what it could be like in 50 or 100 years *because it gets me out of the picture*." [emphasis added]

Many organisations complain about not having enough potential leaders in their leadership pipeline. I think they are looking in the wrong place. The issue isn't with the potential leaders. The issue is with those already in leadership positions who are far more interested in protecting their territory than investing in developing the capability of others.

I once heard a senior leader, who really gets stewardship, describe the role of a leader in relation to his or her people as this: "*Know* them and *grow* them." This is an incredibly powerful concept and one that Yves Tournier✶ has embraced. When I asked him what one of his biggest leadership challenges was to date, he said, "Overcoming my ego, accepting that others can be better than me and so putting them in a situation to grow, develop themselves, and to discover not only what they have deep inside, but their capability to do things they didn't even imagine."

Devon Symister✶ put it this way, "I believe that we should all be working ourselves out of a job. When we do that, we all grow, achieve more, and create new opportunities." Peter Matthews✶ adds, "Too many leaders get caught up in the position and want to keep the role at all costs."

Leaders playing the Ego Game are not interested in knowing their people or growing them. It's too hard. It's a waste of time. It's unnecessary. When they do grow them, it's primarily for the purpose of using them or furthering their own agenda. The sad thing is that they do not realise how much they are limiting the capability of the entire organisation.

Grow your people, and you grow your business in a sustainable way. That's what happens when you are committed to stewardship.

How many leaders do you know who are intentionally building the capacity of others? How many leaders do you know who are invested in developing the capacity of the next generation of leaders? How much time do you invest in knowing and growing others?

When you are committed to stewardship as a way of leading, you create an environment where everyone believes the organisation is theirs to create. You create an environment where people are invested in the purpose of the organisation. You create an environment where choices and autonomy are systematically moved to where the bulk of the work is done.

Becoming a Leader Who Has Earned the Right to Govern

At the end of Chapter 3, it became clear that if you want to be a resilient, engaging, and transformational leader, one who leads with purpose, authenticity, and courage, then it's essential that you have clear, compelling, and congruent values, live with an optimistic worldview, intentionally cultivate rewarding habits, and purposefully nurture empowering beliefs.

This way of being allows you to connect with the heart of leadership, which is stewardship – a commitment to service over self-interest. It is a commitment that motivates us to wisely and courageously distribute and use our power for the good of our teams, the good of our organisations, the good of our communities, and the good of our environments. This perspective means we do not see leadership as a right, but as a

The Heart of Leadership

responsibility. A responsibility that requires us to play a different game of leadership, one where the currency isn't control or coercion or power. It's a responsibility that enables you to become a leader who has earned the right to govern. As Jo Ferreday✷ made clear to me, "This isn't about not making tough decisions as a leader, but about making decisions that are truly for the greater good."

CORE Leaders know that they don't gain the deep respect of others by virtue of their position, or authority, or intelligence, or superiority, but by connecting with the true heart of leadership – stewardship. A commitment to empowerment over control and service over self-interest.

These are also the sort of leaders who pursue and display the real currency of leadership.

It's now time to turn our attention to that.

QUESTIONS FOR REFLECTION

1. What is more typical of your leadership mindset and style – leadership is a right, or leadership is a responsibility?

2. In what ways do you intentionally distribute power to others for the greater good of your team, organisation, or community?

3. Would those around you describe your leadership approach as empowering or controlling?

4. Have you shown a greater commitment to service or to self-interest in the way you live and lead?

CHAPTER 5

The Currency of Leadership

"Leadership is a potent combination of strategy and character. But if you must be without one, be without the strategy."
- NORMAN SCHWARZKOPF

Who are some of the best leaders you have worked with, known, or read about? And what is it about them that stands out to you?

I asked these two questions of all the leaders I interviewed. Their answers were varied and yet incredibly insightful. I would like to share a selection with you.

"Mahatma Gandhi, because of what characterized him i.e., his humility, simplicity, respect, non-violence, etc ... Also, his overall behaviour and the fact that he applied to himself the principles he advocated. This is key!" - YVES TOURNIER

"My mum. She went through so many challenges and created a platform for my siblings and I to be our best selves." - CHARLES SEKWALOR

"Ken Allen, former CEO of DHL Express. He took on a massive challenge and turned things around in the business and invigorated it. He held a long-term belief about what the culture of the organisation should be - one that is ultimately about helping people to become the best they can be."
- PAUL GRAHAM

"Wangari Muta Maathai. She was a renowned Kenyan social, environmental, and political activist, and the first African woman to receive the Nobel Peace Prize for her contribution to sustainable development, democracy, women's rights, and peace. I remember hearing her say, 'You have to have a purpose that is way bigger than you.' "
- AMRI JOHNSON

"Kofi Annan or Mother Teresa. They both showed that influence isn't about power or popularity but about who you are." - ANDY AYIM

The Currency of Leadership

"Stephen Lloyd, Managing Partner of a headhunting firm. The thing I really loved about him was that he was intelligent, very humble, always thinking about new and innovative ways of doing things. He was at the vanguard of social finance. For someone so capable, he always looked you in the eye and was incredibly encouraging. He had this wonderful balance in his life, amazing drive and treated everyone with the utmost respect and dignity." - IAN JOSEPH

"Jacinda Ardern, Prime Minister of New Zealand. Her response to the communities following the terrorist attacks in Christ Church, New Zealand was exceptional. She's someone who is able to speak about what New Zealand stands for. She's not only an amazing orator, but also translates that into tangible outcomes and is able to capture the mood of the people." - WENDY CARTWRIGHT

"Jim Kelleher. He was the most humble General Counsel that I've ever met. He never shot the messenger. With him you always felt like he'd got your back. He never really forgot who he was and where he came from. He never approached discussions from a place of authority. He had a very deeply ingrained sense of who he is. He cared about people at a human level." - DAMON HART

"Paul Kagame, President of Rwanda. He continues to demonstrate selflessness and a commitment to fighting for the broader interests of the people."
– AMADOU DIALLO

"Satya Nadella, current CEO of Microsoft. He's someone who leads in a very humane way. He lives with brokenness in his family and is able to communicate with a lot of empathy and respect."
– LILY MANOHARAN

Unsurprisingly, quite a few people mentioned South Africa's first black head of state and the first president elected in a fully representative democratic election.

"That's an easy answer. Nelson Mandela. Not only because of his resilience and focus on one mission, but because of his ability to build common ground amongst so many people." - JP PERRAUD

"Nelson Mandela. He stood for something. He believed in the value of all lives not just a few. He believed in it to the point that it cost him a lot. Everyone says they stand for something but at what cost? There's a lot of pressure to fold as a leader. Nelson Mandela was one of those leaders who stood for what was right no matter the cost."
– LEE HENDERSON

> "People like Nelson Mandela who went on an extremely rigorous personal journey and was able to bring the nation together. Look at his history he didn't start that way. His journey was painful and yet showed a very clear process of character formation." - CHARLES MCLACHLAN

There is so much more where that came from.

I am sure you recognise some of the leaders that were mentioned. Others may be unknown to you. Regardless, they all have one thing in common. They were, and some still are, leaders who displayed the currency of leadership – character.

Getting Under the Skin of Character

If you asked anyone in a team, or organisation, or country, in almost any context, if they prefer to have a leader with or without character, you would struggle to find someone who does not overwhelmingly want a leader *with* character.

The question must then be asked, what is character?

Many would describe it in terms of how a person behaves or their qualities, but there is so much more to it. The word has its roots in the ancient Greek word *kharaktêr*, which means chisel or stamping tool. It conveys the idea that you create and forge a desired item by intentionally shaping and removing the junk or unwanted material.

So, when we think of a leader with character, we really mean one who has undergone the uncomfortable, sometimes even painful, process of getting rid of undesirable qualities and becoming a person who can be described with words like tenacious, trustworthy, resilient, reliable, courageous, authentic, personal, selfless, full of integrity, or purpose-driven rather than ego-driven.

Jim Loehr adds even more to this picture in his book *Leading with Character*. He describes two types of character – performance character and moral character. **Performance character competencies** drive *'what'* we achieve and support high achievement regardless of whether you cross moral lines or not, and they include focus, persistence, positivity, resilience, decisiveness, fortitude, tough-mindedness, etc. **Moral character competencies** drive *'how'* we achieve what we achieve and support ethical behaviour and enhanced moral judgement and reasoning. These moral character competencies reflect the values we hold and the way we treat others, and include honesty, compassion, integrity, empathy, selflessness, etc.

It goes without saying that leading with moral or ethical character is crucial for leaders who want to increase their positive impact and create a long-lasting legacy.

Why does any of this matter? Why does character matter in leadership? Why does moral character matter?

The Currency of Leadership

The devastation to our economy, our organisations, and the personal lives of many leaders described in Chapter 1 should answer those questions. It paints a picture of the severe impact of a crisis of character in leaders who were unable to connect with what their people were really thinking, feeling, and experiencing. They were unable to hear their people at the level of their hearts. They did not have the character to use their power for the good of others.

I would like to add one more answer to the reason why character, especially moral character, matters in leadership by stepping back in time – more than 130 years back in time, to be precise.

It's 1888. A Swedish chemist, who made his fortune inventing and producing dynamite, and was the holder of 355 patents, was reading a newspaper and suddenly came across a headline and story that rocked him to his core.

What was so shocking and discouraging?

Well, the story was meant to be an obituary about his brother, Ludvig, who had recently died from a heart attack in Cannes, France. Instead, the obituary in the French newspaper was about him. The editor had mixed up the brothers. The headline read, "*Le marchand de la mort est mort*" ("The merchant of death is dead"). The scathing obituary about Dr. Alfred Nobel went on to describe a man who had amassed riches by helping people find more ways to kill one another faster than ever before.

This summary of his life shocked him. Was this his life legacy? Was this what he was known for? It is believed that from that moment onwards, he resolved to use his wealth to change his legacy.

In a sense, Alfred Nobel had a unique opportunity to live his life all over again and do it right. To live a life that counted.

The Nobel Prize awards we have today – recipients of which include Martin Luther King Jr., Marie Curie, Nelson Mandela, Barack Obama, Wangari Maathai, Liu Xiaobo – exist thanks to the more than SEK 31 million (today approximately £145 million) Nobel left after his death in 1896 to fund awards for people whose work benefits humanity.

As leaders, if we are really honest, **we want our lives to count.** When all is said and done, we want what we did with our lives to have made a difference, not only to our organisations but to our families and even our communities.

The challenge is not to get sucked into the false notion that we can rely on our authority or power to lead, without putting in the hard work of growing in character. When we fall into that trap, the result is burnout, stress, and ethical and moral lapses.

Many of the greatest collapses in business history (a few of which I described in Chapter 1) have occurred because of failure in character.

The Currency of Leadership

It is no wonder Abraham Lincoln is believed to have said,

> "Nearly all people can stand adversity, but if you want to test a person's character, give them power."

As leaders, we have tremendous power to do good and yet, without intentionally forging a character that curtails our natural propensity for self-interest, we abuse that power and live with the consequences of ethical and moral boundaries crossed all over the place, acting as time bombs ticking away and ready to cause overwhelming devastation – financial crises, lost jobs, racial tension, lost homes, corruption, fraud. The list goes on.

Paul Graham✷ echoed this idea as we discussed some of the challenges leaders face today and the importance of character amongst leaders, "How you achieve success is as important as the success you achieve and yet it's easy to allow bravado to hide the vulnerability in all of us and so everyone misses out."

If it was your obituary, what would people say about you? Would you be described as someone who lived and led with character?

Consider your answer to the following questions:
- What do you do when moral and ethical lines are crossed in your organisation?

- When did you last raise a red flag about behaviour that was not in line with your organisation's values and vision?
- What do you do when you witness injustice or corruption?
- To what degree do you believe that power, purpose, and privilege should be localised in one or a few people within your organisation, your team, your community?
- How intentional are you about dispersing power within your organisation and replacing control with collaboration and cooperation?
- To what degree are you committed to a cause larger than yourself?
- When it comes down to a choice between personal gain and the welfare of others, what choice do you typically make?
- What ethical and moral compromises have you made to ensure financial gain or protect your reputation?
- When you have been under pressure, how strong have your moral muscles (of integrity, honesty, courage, compassion, humility, etc.) proved to be?

These are intentionally tough questions that may very well raise some sobering answers for you.

However, perhaps this question will help you consider where to go next: What helps CORE Leaders develop moral character?

Developing Character that Matters

Hopefully, you are beginning to see the fundamental connection between having a strong and healthy core and the ability to lead with character. Without the self-awareness to develop clear values; without a connection to a meaningful purpose bigger than yourself; without the conviction to live with an optimistic and healthy worldview; without the drive to intentionally cultivate rewarding habits that maximise your energy and positive impact on others; without the commitment to nurture empowering beliefs about yourself, about others, about leadership, you will never develop the moral character needed to live a life that truly matters and stand up for what you believe in – even if it costs you.

In Part 3, we will explore one of the most powerful ways I know to strategically invest in growing specific moral character muscles.

For now, it is important to note that when you dig deep into the stories of those leaders who have become known as men or women who lead with character, you realise that **leading with character is not natural for most of us.** Neither does it simply come about when we face times of adversity. As the late James Lane Allen said, "Adversity doesn't build character. It reveals it." And how correct he was.

Character building doesn't just happen; it requires intention. You are not simply born with qualities like reliability, resilience, integrity; those traits are something you take responsibility for building.

It involves intention. It requires training. It takes a willingness to do the hard work of deciding what we want to be known for, what we stand for, and, if necessary, what we are willing to die for.

Even the great Nelson Mandela's character was not simply forged because he was incarcerated. Here's a reflection he shared after leaving prison, "As I walked out the door toward the gate that would lead to my freedom, I knew if I didn't leave my bitterness and hatred behind, I'd still be in prison."

It involves intention to go through 27 years of imprisonment and come out with a desire to forgive and not hold grudges. It requires training to rise above your personal pain and stand for ideals everybody can connect to. It takes a willingness to maintain high levels of integrity when the alternative, the status quo, would be so much easier.

Our world needs more leaders who are committed to doing the hard work of growing from the inside out as they balance power with the moral character muscles of compassion and integrity.

The Best Way to Lead

One of the fundamental questions this book is determined to answer is, what is the best way to lead? Or to be even more specific: what is the best way to lead others so that you win their hearts and minds and unleash the best of their productivity, motivation, and engagement towards worthwhile goals that achieve good for all?

If I was forced to use one word to answer that question based on everything I have said so far, it would be this – **influence**. Yet so many leaders have misunderstood influence and how to grow it. They really need to pay attention to the words of Erwin McManus in *Chasing Daylight*:

> "Influence is about winning the heart and soul of another person through the strength of your own character. Influence flows through relationships. Influence can do what command can never do. Influence is born out of who a person is. Influence is rooted in character."

Perhaps the reason so many leaders prefer to rely on their power, authority, or intelligence as the currency of their leadership rather than relying on the strength of their moral character, is that deep down, because they haven't done the hard work, they realise they will have very little influence to inspire, motivate, and engage others otherwise. And yet, the sort of leadership that wins hearts and minds, the sort of leadership that brings out the best in those around us, the sort of leadership that earns respect, increases engagement, and enhances productivity is not leadership based on power, authority, or intelligence, but character-based leadership.

CORE Leaders have embraced this type of leadership. They understand that if you want to lead in a way that stands the test of time and really makes a difference, then you need to focus on your influence and remember that influence has everything to do with your character.

QUESTIONS FOR REFLECTION

1. Who are some of the best leaders you have worked with, known, or read about? To what degree would you describe them as people of character?

2. What do you rely most on in the way you lead – position, authority, intelligence, or character?

3. Which of the questions on pages 105/106 did you find most challenging? What does that reveal about the current strength of your moral character?

4. In what ways do you see the need to grow in moral character? What difference would that make to your leadership?

PART 3

How You Can Develop a Strong Core

"If people knew how hard I had to work to gain my mastery, it would not seem so wonderful at all."
- MICHELANGELO

CHAPTER 6

Prepare to Transform

"Transformation is a process, not an event."
- JOHN P. KOTTER

So far, on our journey together, we have explored some of the secrets of the best, most engaging, most resilient, most courageous, and transformational leaders on the planet:

- They are committed to playing the Service Game.
- They relate to others in a way that unleashes the best of their motivation, passion, creativity, and energy towards a worthwhile goal.
- They put in the hard work of leading from the inside out.

- They have clear values that act as guiding coordinates for their lives and ground themselves in what they stand for.
- They live with an optimistic worldview that guides their decisions and helps them and others to thrive, even in challenging times.
- They cultivate rewarding mental, behavioural, and attitudinal habits that maximise their energy, courage, and impact.
- They intentionally surface and overcome shadow beliefs, and they nurture beliefs that empower themselves and others.
- They live out stewardship as the heart of their leadership, demonstrating a greater commitment to empowerment over control and service over self-interest.
- They display, embrace, and pursue moral character growth as the currency of their leadership.

These secrets help the best leaders, CORE Leaders, to maximise their energy, increase their impact, and build their resilience.

It's now time to get really practical and discover how you can develop the sort of internal structure and resilience necessary to live and lead with more purpose, authenticity, courage, and effectiveness than you ever dared to believe.

Prepare to Transform

Let's start by pulling the curtains back on what is truly involved in any personal transformation and growth journey.

From Caterpillar to Butterfly

I really wish I could say that the journey of becoming our best selves, the journey of becoming the best leader we could be, the journey of personal transformation was an easy one, but it isn't. In case I have not alluded to this enough times already, it's hard work. Learning and unlearning is hard work. Becoming a CORE Leader is hard work. However, the payoff is huge.

I have come to think of the journey of personal transformation very much like the journey a caterpillar goes through on its path to becoming a butterfly. There are some necessary steps and components you cannot circumvent. If you try, you do so at your peril. This story by Paulo Coelho, author of *The Alchemist*, illustrates what I mean…

> "A man spent hours watching a butterfly struggling to emerge from its cocoon. It managed to make a small hole, but its body was too large to get through it. After a long struggle, it appeared to be exhausted and remained absolutely still.
>
> The man decided to help the butterfly and, with a pair of scissors, he cut open the cocoon (chrysalis),

thus releasing the butterfly. However, the butterfly's body was very small and wrinkled and its wings were all crumpled.

The man continued to watch, hoping that, at any moment, the butterfly would open its wings and fly away. Nothing happened; in fact, the butterfly spent the rest of its brief life dragging around its shrunken body and shrivelled wings, incapable of flight.

What the man - out of kindness and his eagerness to help - had failed to understand was that the tight cocoon and the efforts that the butterfly had to make in order to squeeze out of that tiny hole were Nature's way of training the butterfly and of strengthening its wings."

Coelho summarises the story by saying, "Sometimes, a little extra effort is precisely what prepares us for the next obstacle to be faced. Anyone who refuses to make that effort, or gets the wrong sort of help, is left unprepared to fight the next battle and never manages to fly off to their destiny."

This powerful story reinforces **the importance of struggle and effort** in any transformation journey. Yet there is more to all of this that is relevant for us as leaders because it only highlights the final stages of the caterpillar's transformation.

Prepare to Transform

Amazingly, scientists have discovered that the radical transformation from caterpillar entails a complete breakdown of all its tissues. To be more specific, the caterpillar releases some digestive enzymes that literally break down its body and turn it into a protein-rich caterpillar soup. Once the caterpillar has disintegrated all its tissues except for the imaginal discs, those discs use the protein-rich soup all around them to fuel the rapid cell division required to form the wings, antennae, legs, eyes, genitals and all the other features of an adult butterfly.

What has that got to do with the journey we are on and our growth as leaders?

Well, the reason I think the caterpillar's radical metamorphosis is analogous to the personal transformation we need to go on as leaders is that we too need to intentionally strip away and, metaphorically speaking, destroy old ways of thinking, seeing, believing, and behaving in order to take on new ways of thinking, seeing, believing, and behaving.

Physiologically, that means creating new neural pathways in our brains that ignite new behaviours, new attitudes, and new beliefs. The challenge, of course, is that our old ways of believing, thinking, and behaving as leaders will not give up without a fight. The mental, emotional, and physical habits that you have developed to date won't let you strip them off easily. They will want to hold you firmly and resolutely in a caterpillar world instead of letting you fly off to your destiny of leading in a more purposeful, courageous, and transformational way.

3 Truths You Need to Know About Personal Transformation

There are three things you need to know and embrace about personal transformation. They will help you succeed in achieving a breakthrough in your personal and leadership growth:

1. Resistance Is Guaranteed

If you were going to the gym to work out and get fit, there is no way you would grow without resistance. The same thing applies when you are growing as a leader and as a person. It's essential that you anticipate resistance and prepare to push through it. There will be resistance to new ideas. There will be resistance to letting go of old ways of thinking. It is absolutely par for the course.

2. It Takes Time

I would love to be able to offer you a 'matrix-style' blue or red pill that would immediately turn you into a CORE Leader, but no such pill exists. There are no shortcuts. And if anyone is offering an easy road, I promise it will only lead to shallow roots in your life and leadership. It takes time to figure out your core values. It takes time to overcome old habits that have been holding you back and to cultivate the right, rewarding habits that will maximise your energy, courage, and impact. It takes time to uncover limiting beliefs and nurture empowering ones.

3. It Is Possible

It's difficult, it takes time, and it requires effort, but it is absolutely possible to grow. It is possible to experience a transformation in your life, in your perspective, and in your leadership so that you can lead from a place of purpose, authenticity, and courage. Others have gone before us, and thankfully, they have not covered up the path.

The Oxygen Mask Rule of Leadership

As we continue to think about strengthening our internal core as leaders, another important image to hold in mind is the safety demonstration and announcement on airplane flights. You know what I'm talking about. It's the moment when the regular air travellers among us are tempted to switch off because we have heard them so many times. It always brings a smile to my face when the flight attendant says, "Should the cabin lose pressure, oxygen masks will drop from the overhead area. Please place the mask over your own mouth and nose before assisting others, including young children."

Their message is this – **make sure you are at your best in order to be able to give your best to others**, including your loved ones. There couldn't be a more relevant message to leaders in business and in life.

In their book *Living Forward*, Daniel Harkavy and Michael Hyatt have this to say about the absolute importance of self-leadership, "You can't take care of anyone else unless you first take care of yourself... You are in a much better position to serve others when your basic needs are met and your 'tank is full.'" The sobering truth is that too many leaders are running on empty. Empty on clear values. Empty on an optimistic worldview. Empty on rewarding habits. Empty on empowering beliefs. Empty on moral character.

If you want to lead with greater levels of purpose, authenticity, courage, and effectiveness, then you need to be a leader who puts their own oxygen mask on first.

Remember, you cannot give what you do not have.

Putting My Oxygen Mask On

For the leaders I interviewed, there was a wide array of approaches to applying the oxygen mask rule – spending time with family, listening to podcasts, working out, engaging in sports, not reading emails at weekends, meditating, praying, reading books, and more.

I would like to give you an idea of what it looks like for me.

A few years ago, on a business trip to Florida, I had one of the best long-haul flights of my life. How come? It wasn't the food, as good as that was. It wasn't the safety demonstration, though, yes, I did smile when

Prepare to Transform

the flight attendant talked about oxygen masks. It wasn't the service, though that was ace. It wasn't even that this particular Boeing plane had one of the best flat-beds in the skies. What was it then? Well, during what was the culmination of an intense and busy few weeks, I got to do two of my favourite things – read a book and write in my journal.

Not only was I filling up my internal tank as I made time for a bit of self-renewal (one of the six rewarding habits we will explore in Chapter 9), but the book I was reading and journaling about was the *New York Times* bestseller by Greg McKeown, *Essentialism: The Disciplined Pursuit of Less*.

In *Essentialism*, McKeown sets out the premise that doing less but better is the key to maximising our impact and success. This is more challenging than most people and leaders think. It has certainly been a major challenge for me.

At that point in my life, I was extremely busy. I was working with an amazing team of talented individuals, helping global clients maximise their performance and growth through engaging and developing their people and their leaders. It was a demanding role, but I relished the day-to-day opportunity to do incredible work. My wife and I were balancing the equally vibrant schedules of our three boys. There were appointments and activities with friends and family to fit in. Oh, and did I mention that my wife and I were house-hunting at that time? That brought with it its own host of challenges and decisions. What area? What school? Is this the right time to move the boys? The list went on.

As I considered the busyness of my life, **I had to accept that I couldn't do it all.** I had to make trade-offs. And McKeown's book provided terrific insight and guidance on how to do that with intentionality and with wisdom.

Every day we make decisions about what to focus on and where to invest our time, energy, and resources. This applies to individuals and organisations alike. Our focus shifts from one key decision to another, often without us even realising it:

- Diversify our product offering or simplify our existing products?
- Chinese or Caribbean for dinner?
- Open the new office in New York or Milan?
- Spend time with the kids or work late?
- Tidy the house or pay a cleaner?
- Cross ethical lines or raise a red flag?

What makes things really interesting is that **our decisions always require trade-offs**. That is why it is so important to **be crystal clear about what matters most in our lives and be clear about our core values** – the guiding principles for our life and leadership.

For leaders, that means asking questions like, "How

Prepare to Transform

do I know and grow my people?" "How do I enable and empower my people to be at their best?" and following through on the answers.

For me, that meant asking myself the question, "What is it that only I can do?" For example, only I can be a husband to my wife, or father to my boys, or set out a clear vision for my team.

Asking that question helped me work out what to delegate or even eliminate from my to-do list and schedule.

We live in a world where being busy is a badge of honour and there is always more on the to-do list than is realistic. However, as I read that book, I realised that one of the secrets to success, operating at our highest point of contribution, is not cramming our schedules with more or trying to do it all. **The secret is doing less, not more, less and better.** Not an easy feat, but one we must all master if we want to maximise success, professionally or personally.

These are a couple of strategies I apply to achieve that:

- Schedule a personal quarterly retreat to review my life plan and update my personal goals for the next quarter
- Live a life true to my voice of purpose within
- Pause before saying 'Yes'
- Say 'No' more often, firmly, and resolutely, yet gracefully

- Recognise that I make a trade-off with every decision
- Consider what I want to go big on in terms of the projects that I get involved in – where do I want to hedge my bets?
- Build more thinking and reflection time into my schedule – with key questions to support my reflection

CORE Leaders don't leave their growth and development to chance. They are intentional about putting their oxygen mask on first.

Get Ready for a Breakthrough

If you started a fitness regime, would you expect to develop increased muscle strength overnight? Anyone that has done any fitness training or knows how the body works will offer a resounding and overwhelming, "No!". Research and experience show that it takes anywhere between three to six months of dedicated training to increase the strength of our physical muscles.

The same applies when it comes to developing and strengthening our internal core of mental and character muscles. It takes effort, intentionality, and time to experience the growth we need to become resilient, engaging, and transformational leaders.

Likewise, in the same way that physical muscles

Prepare to Transform

atrophy when they are not used for prolonged periods of time, we have to continuously train our mental and moral character muscles. This means that building the character muscles and neurological architecture to support them takes time and must be seen as a lifelong process.

While the categories of fitness training are broadly set – cardio, resistance, free weights, etc. – the options and combinations that exist within those categories are as varied as there are bodies on this planet.

For example, training for maximum strength requires lifting heavy weights in limited repetitions, while improving explosive strength requires moving light-to-moderate weights as fast as possible. Or training for endurance, like a marathon, relies upon aerobic efficiency to supply oxygen and nutrients to the working muscles while removing metabolic waste.

In the next four chapters, we will build on what we discovered about the four CORE attributes in Part 2 (Clear values, Optimistic worldview, Rewarding habits, Empowering beliefs). I will share some of the most effective strategies, tools, and ideas for working out, developing, and strengthening your internal core in each of the four areas.

Get ready for a personal leadership breakthrough.

QUESTIONS FOR REFLECTION

1. Are you intentional about growing as a leader, or do you typically leave it to chance and opportunity?

2. How comfortable are you with putting your oxygen mask on as a leader?

3. In what areas of life and leadership do you already recognise that you need to experience a breakthrough?

CHAPTER 7

Align Your Life Around Clear Values

"Let us endeavour so to live that when we come to die even the undertaker will be sorry."

- MARK TWAIN

To ensure your values are overwhelmingly clear, congruent, and compelling, we will focus on one of the most powerful ways to strategically invest in growing your internal core and specific moral character muscles. But first, let me ask you a question: What is your leadership philosophy and how does it integrate with your overall life plan?

If you don't have a plan that you can share with me or if you can't recite your philosophy from memory, that tells me you are at the mercy of the leadership philosophies of those around you – good or bad.

And, in case you think that it's not necessary to have a clearly articulated and personal leadership philosophy that is aligned with the best version of yourself, then please re-read Chapter 1, slowly. Or consider these words from the Russian-American writer and philosopher Ayn Rand:

"As a human being, you have no choice about the fact that you need a philosophy. Your only choice is whether you define your philosophy by a conscious, rational, disciplined process of thought and scrupulously logical deliberation – or let your subconscious accumulate a junk heap of unwarranted conclusions, false generalisations, undefined contradictions, undigested slogans, unidentified wishes, doubts and fears, thrown together by chance, but integrated by your subconscious into a kind of mongrel philosophy and fused into a single, solid weight: self-doubt. Like a ball and chain in the place where your mind's wings should have grown."

It is essential that you have a philosophy, aligned to your best self, that guides the way you live and lead. It should incorporate your most important values, mindset, habits, and beliefs. You either have one you have worked on and intentionally integrated into your life, or, in Rand's hard-hitting words, you have a mongrel philosophy that shapes your life as it pleases. The choice is yours. There is no middle ground.

Align Your Life Around Clear Values

My own philosophy has taken years of intentional reflection, introspection, and crafting. I call it 'Obi's Empowering, Limitless Story'. I have memorised all 899 words, which describe my life purpose, my vision and values, my worldview, the rewarding habits that matter most to me and give me the most energy, my most empowering beliefs, and the performance and moral character muscles that are critical for achieving my life vision.

I also have an accompanying life plan that I started developing in 2011 and have been tweaking and refining ever since. It now includes additional elements, such as the eight life categories I focus on to ensure I'm living my best life and the annual goals that support each of those categories. I review this regularly – weekly, monthly, quarterly, and during my annual personal retreat. I have also shared it with close friends, who help keep me accountable to the vision I have for my life and how I want to show up in the world – as a person, as a husband, as a father, as a businessman, and as a leader.

At those times in my life when I lost my way, my life plan and my empowering, limitless story have played a significant role in helping me get back on track. And so, as we progress through the next four chapters, we will keep returning to these strategic documents.

Now we're ready to focus on the first key part of your life and leadership philosophy – **clear values**.

There are three things you need to do clarify your values:

1. Know what you want to be remembered for
2. Know your why
3. Ignite the fire within

Let's take a closer look at each one.

How Do You Want to be Remembered?

At the beginning of this book, I said these insights and strategies will not only make a difference to your leadership, but also to the way you live. They will make a difference to your marriage, your parenting, your relationships with family and friends, even your relationship with neighbours.

They will make a difference because these ideas are ultimately about leaving a life and leadership legacy that you and your loved ones can be proud of.

"Our legacy," says Michael Hyatt in *Living Forward*, "comprises the spiritual, intellectual, relational, vocational, and social capital we pass on. It's the sum total of the beliefs you embrace, the values you live by, the love you express and the service you render to others. It's the you-shaped stamp you leave when you go."

When my second son was about six years old, he had this obsession with the number 100. As I drove him to school one day, he said, "Dad, you're going to live to be

Align Your Life Around Clear Values

100!" I laughed and imagined what that would be like. I am 30 years older than him, so I joked about the two of us walking around with Zimmer frames.

Shortly afterwards, it got me thinking seriously about my legacy and my death. What would I want my family to say about me when I die? I had been considering this since I was 18, not because I'm morbid, but because it is one of the activities Stephen Covey asks readers to do in his book *7 Habits of Highly Effective People*. However, I couldn't remember ever writing it down. The exercise is to imagine you are at your own funeral. Loved ones and friends and colleagues are there. You are listening in on the conversations and hearing what people say about you. What would you want them to say?

I have now written my eulogy. Two, in fact. One from the perspective of my kids, and the other from my wife's perspective. [She is not too keen on that, by the way.] I have added them to my life plan because I want to live with the end in mind. I want to live life with clarity about what it is I am on this planet for. I want to live my life with and on purpose.

Here is a snippet of my eulogy from the perspective of my boys:

> "Our Dad had a positive impact on a lot of people's lives, including ours. He was very intentional about fathering us in a way that touched all areas

of our lives - when we were young boys, he was a wrestling partner, punching bag, comforter, teacher, and coach, and as we grew up, he also became a friend, mentor, advisor, and so much more, but, above all, we remember him as a father to the end - totally committed to our spiritual, emotional, psychological, and physical growth and well-being."

In case you didn't realise, one of my life categories and core values is to be a purposeful father and, therefore, I have written this eulogy with a very clear direction in mind. I don't get it perfect, but I am living with the end in mind, and I am able to course correct when I get off track.

How do you want to be remembered by the people you love and those you have worked with? Answering this question and writing down the answer will absolutely clarify what you want to stand for in life and at work.

What's Your WHY?

It's been said, "When you lose your why, you lose your way." So, what's your WHY? I love the way Simon Sinek, author of *Start With Why*, defines this: "Your WHY is the cause, the belief, the purpose that inspires you." I think I discovered my WHY while watching a three-part series called *Return to Eden* when I was seven years old. To cut a long story short, in the movie a doctor performs plastic surgery on the main female character after she is thrown in a crocodile-infested swamp by her cheating, money-hungry husband and almost mauled to death by a crocodile.

I remember thinking that doctors seem to bring out the best in people and I wanted to do something like that. It sowed within me a belief that you and I have the potential within us to contribute something unique to the world that no one else could. It laid a foundation for me, discovering a purpose to help leaders grow in their personal mastery so that they can live transformed lives, which in turn leads to a better world.

When your WHY is fully aligned with your best self, you tap into an energy that enables you to grow the mental and moral character strength to excel in your leadership. "Money is important, but it's not a big motivator. Purpose is what does it for me," says Mathias Lingnau✶. For Luke Manning✶, this is the key to being able to navigate many of the pressures that leaders face, "Knowing your why and bigger purpose is where it all begins if you want to be a resilient leader."

Ignite the Fire Within

In the movie *Cinderella Man*, inspired by the life story of James J. Braddock, Russell Crowe plays the role of Braddock, who is an incredible up-and-coming boxer terrorising everyone that comes his way. Braddock ends up having a chronic hand problem that means he loses some of his fights, and subsequently all of his winnings and investments during the Great Depression of the 1930s. He goes from being an incredible fighter to living off social assistance, literally living hand to mouth. Through several twists and turns, he ends up with an opportunity to have one last fight and earn some extra money to put food on the table. He goes into the fight as the underdog, underrated and unappreciated. To everyone's surprise, not only does he win that fight, but he also recovers his boxing licence and makes it all the way to the heavyweight championship. True to life, on June 13, 1935, James Braddock causes one of the greatest upsets in the history of boxing by defeating heavyweight champion Max Bear.

In the film, during one of his critical fights in the lead up to the championship event, his coach exhorts him with these words, "You've got to fight this from the inside out. From the inside out!"

I've watched that film several times, and that particular scene even more. Why? Well, for one thing, it's a reminder that so much of our performance and impact begins with developing the right internal and mental climate.

To become the best leader you can be, you must know what you're living for, what you're fighting for, and even what you're willing to die for. And that is an inside out game.

I have three boys and grew up without a father. So one of the things I am fighting for is to be a father who enables his boys to thrive, make the most of their God-given talents, and leave a positive mark on our world.

What ignites your fire? What are you fighting for?

Rediscovering Your Way

Have you ever asked yourself this question, "What does it mean to be human?" For some leaders that question is way too deep and esoteric. They prefer staying on the surface. They prefer focusing on tasks, results, activities, achievements, and action.

I'm all about results. I'm all for achievements. I'm definitely for action. I wouldn't be writing this book if I wasn't. But I am interested in these things in a way that stays true to the beauty of our humanity and doesn't strip us of it. A lot of leaders are not really in touch with their humanity, and therefore, they are not in touch with the hearts and minds of those they lead.

Knowing what you want to be remembered for, knowing your why, and knowing what you're living and fighting for will help you connect with your humanity. Connecting with your humanity will give you more clarity about your values and purpose, fuelling you with greater levels of resilience as you engage with others each day.

If you really want to thrive as leader, if you really want to win hearts and minds, if you really want to make a difference in this world, you need to be willing to go deep and connect with what it means to be truly human and truly alive.

As I said in Part 2, when you have clear values, you can easily course correct, stay anchored, and leave a legacy that counts.

As leaders, when we have lost our way, the path towards a life of purpose, impact, and resilience begins with reconnecting to our humanity, reconnecting to our deepest values, and capturing that as part of our personal leadership philosophy.

However, when it comes to crafting your leadership philosophy and life plan, this is only the beginning. There is so much more.

Align Your Life Around Clear Values

QUESTIONS FOR REFLECTION

1. If your life were turned into an inspiring movie, what is the script – the empowering story – you would like to send to the producers?

2. What do you want to be remembered for by your family, loved ones, friends, business partners, and colleagues?

3. What is your WHY?

4. What are you fighting for and what gets you out of bed in the morning that fuels you to make a difference as a leader?

5. What does it mean to be in touch with your humanity as you lead others? What changes do you need to make to the way you lead as you connect more with your incredible human potential and that of others?

CHAPTER 8

Live with an Optimistic Worldview

*"If you change the way you look at things,
the things you look at change."*
- WAYNE DYER

I love this poem by Walter Wintle. It is the perfect illustration of the power of our mindset or worldview.

*"If you think you are beaten, you are
If you think you dare not, you don't,
If you like to win, but you think you can't
It is almost certain you won't.*

*If you think you'll lose, you're lost
For out of the world we find,
Success begins with a fellow's will
It's all in the state of mind.*

> If you think you are outclassed, you are
> You've got to think high to rise,
> You've got to be sure of yourself before
> You can ever win a prize.
>
> Life's battles don't always go
> To the stronger or faster man,
> But soon or late the man who wins
> Is the man WHO THINKS HE CAN!"

World-renowned Stanford University psychologist Carol Dweck, who has conducted decades of research on achievement, success, and mindset, would wholeheartedly agree with Walter Wintle. She says, "We like to think of our champions and idols as superheroes who were born different from us. We don't like to think of them as relatively ordinary people who made themselves extraordinary." And how did they make themselves extraordinary? Through their mindset and worldview.

Gilles Acogny★ shared this with me, "Resilience starts with a strong mindset and the ability to not give into external circumstances."

As a leader, embracing the challenges you face, believing the best is yet to come, and putting the work in are incredible ways of developing an optimistic worldview that enables you to continue to maximise your energy, increase your impact, and build your resilience.

Live with an Optimistic Worldview

How else do you develop this mindset and way of seeing the world?

There are four ways to foster and live with an optimistic worldview:

1. Zero in on compelling goals
2. Learn from every challenge and failure
3. Value your pain
4. Embrace the struggle

Let us look at each one in detail.

Zero In on Compelling Goals

What is a goal? In simple terms, **a goal is a dream with a deadline.** So much has been written about goals and goal-setting over the years, and yet many leaders do not know how to create goals that are truly compelling. I'm talking about the kind of goals that enable them to live and lead with greater levels of purpose, authenticity, and effectiveness. I'm talking about the kind of goals that fuel passion and loyalty in those you lead.

I believe that a major reason for this is that, while many leaders may understand the what and how of goal-setting, they are not really connected with the deeper why.

When I first started dabbling with personal leadership concepts, I heard one of my virtual mentors, Jim Rohn, say this about goals, "The main purpose in setting a goal is what it makes of you to achieve it."

I hope you can appreciate the power in that insight.

Goals have less to do with the actual achievement and much more to do with **the person you become as you achieve that goal**. For example, let's say you have a goal to successfully launch a new product line and grow it to £X million revenue. When you achieve the goal, the real prize is not the £X million. No! The real prize is the person you have become in the process of achieving that goal. That means if, for some strange reason, you lost it all, you would still have all the experience, the insights, the learning, the skills that you have developed along the way. That's why the best leaders zero in on compelling goals. They recognise that the real value isn't external, but within. The real value is the growth and transformation of their worldview. The real value is in the character they develop.

So how do you zero in on compelling goals? By setting CALM goals, which involves asking yourself four key questions:

- **What can I do that will require *Courage*?**

    The best things in life are on the other side of our fears.

- **What can I do that will make me come *Alive*?**

    The late theologian and philosopher Howard Thurman once said, "Don't ask yourself what the world needs. Ask yourself what makes you come alive, and

Live with an Optimistic Worldview

then go do that. Because what the world needs is people who have come alive." Figure out what those things are for you.

- **What can I do that will allow me to *Learn* in the process?**

  Remember, the real value is in who you are becoming and what you are learning along the way. The greater the opportunity for learning, the greater the value in the goal.

- **What can I do that is *Meaningful*?**

  Pursuing goals takes energy and inevitably presents challenges. The more meaningful the goal, the greater the staying power at seeing the goal through, especially during the difficult moments when you are tempted to give up.

Zeroing in on compelling goals is an incredible training ground for stretching your mindset, growing your mental toughness and character, and fostering a view of the world that is enriching, enabling, and resilient. It causes leaders to create opportunities where others never even realised there are some.

Learn from Every Challenge and Failure

The legendary inventor Thomas Edison is thought to be the person who created the light bulb. While he didn't actually create the first one, he certainly made it commercially available and cheap. He and his associates worked on finding the right filament for a long time, so that it would last thousands of hours and become available in our homes. The best sources suggest that it took them 6000 tests just to get the right filament. A reporter once asked him what it felt like to fail thousands of times. His answer was, "I haven't failed thousands of times. It's just taken me thousands of goes to get it right." Thomas Edison was most certainly someone who understood this principle.

As a recovering perfectionist, especially early on in my career, I used to find failures and difficulties really challenging – they hurt my ego. I felt they damaged my reputation. I didn't like the way they made me look. You will notice that it was all "me, me, me."

Most leaders don't enjoy failure. Yet as leadership guru John Maxwell says in *Failing Forward*, "The difference between average people and achieving people is their perception of and response to failure." Gemma Hiett✶ said this to me, "Resilience isn't something you have innately. It's something you build. How you process and make meaning of failure, especially, is one of the key things that either grows your resilience or doesn't."

During my training in neuro-linguistic programming (NLP), I learnt this phrase, "There's no such thing as failure, only feedback." As a leader, some great questions to ask in times of failure or when things have

Live with an Optimistic Worldview

gone majorly wrong are: "What is it about my leadership that may have caused this? What is it about my leadership that is preventing my people from bringing the best of their ideas, passion, creativity and motivation to what we're doing?" When you ask questions like that, **the failure becomes an opportunity to learn** rather than cast blame or even bury your head in the sand.

With this sort of mindset, nothing can be thrown your way that you cannot overcome.

Value Your Pain

Do you like pain? I am hoping your instinctive answer is "No." If not, you might want to see someone about your masochistic tendencies. That said, I'm a big fan of working out at the gym, and I have come to appreciate the phrase, "No pain, no gain." To me, it means hurting muscles are not a sign that something is wrong, but a sign that I am on the right path to growth and fitness. The same can be said of life. Many situations we face are painful, incredibly painful – failed ventures, failed product launches, loved ones going through health challenges, etc. Painful situations are never easy, but they do present incredible opportunities for growth.

Most people don't become who they want because they are too attached to who they have been. And that is because **most people want the convenience of**

transformation without the inconvenience of pain. And yet, as Melanie Eusebe✶ said to me, "Resilience is something that comes out of the dark times that you push and suffer through. In order to know the light, you must know the darkness." Hannah Martin✶ put it this way, "When you've been through something tough and learned from it, you have a strength that no one can take away from you."

There is tremendous value to be gained from the painful situations we face when we adopt the right mindset and worldview. It is important that you take the time to mine the valleys and learn the lessons that bitter seasons can teach you. That is a sure path to living with an optimistic worldview.

Embrace the Struggle

In Chapter 6, I talked about the fierce struggle that a caterpillar must endure on its transformation journey to becoming a butterfly. That necessary struggle is Nature's way of preparing it to thrive in its new world. The same is true for us. As Max Ward✶ described it to me, "If you feel leadership is going to be a walk in the park, then you're not doing the real work that needs to be done. I don't know of any successful leader who hasn't been through the dark night of the soul. I think it's a rite of passage."

If we are not struggling, we are not learning. In

Live with an Optimistic Worldview

fact, neuroscientists have found that mistakes and challenges are helpful for brain growth. Not only is struggle good for our brains, but leaders who know about the value of struggle also improve their learning potential. They know that struggle is one of the best opportunities to grow in mental toughness, resilience, and character. They don't see life as happening *to* them but *for* them. This enables them to hold on to that optimistic worldview no matter the circumstances.

A Different View of the World

It's no wonder CORE Leaders see the best in others. It's no wonder CORE Leaders earn the deep respect of others and unleash the best in them during the good times *and* the extremely tough times. They have a different way of looking at the world. No matter what they're going through, good can come out of it. The best is yet to come and, for many, this is reflected in their leadership philosophy and life plan. Not only have they aligned their lives around clear values, but they also zero in on compelling goals, embracing the learning, challenges, pain, and struggle that will inevitably come their way.

QUESTIONS FOR REFLECTION

1. Review some of the goals you are currently working on. Are they compelling goals? What changes would you need to make to ensure they are CALM (Courage, Alive, Learn, Meaningful)?

2. What challenges are you facing right now that are perfect training grounds for you to grow in mental toughness, resilience, and character?

3. In what ways do you need to start seeing failures and challenges as feedback and as an opportunity to learn and grow?

4. When you are going through a painful situation, how can you use the pain to make a greater contribution as a leader instead of wasting the struggle?

CHAPTER 9

Cultivate Rewarding Habits

*"Motivation is what gets you started.
Habit is what keeps you going."*
- JIM ROHN

CORE Leaders are committed to intentionally cultivating mental, behavioural, attitudinal habits that maximise their energy, their resilience, their attitude, their courage, and their impact every day. But why do you need habits? And why do you need to be intentional about cultivating the right ones? Because habits give you leverage.

There are many things in life we just can't do or achieve on our own without applying the power of leverage. Many of us apply this principle when buying a new home – we leverage financial resources from banks. Many of us apply this principle when seeking new job and business opportunities – we leverage our networks.

The same applies to achieving a breakthrough in our leadership effectiveness. **You need to leverage new insights, new skills, and new strategies.** You may even need to leverage coaching or mentoring from others to achieve a breakthrough.

Herman Stewart✶, author of *Every Child Needs a Mentor*, knows a thing or two about the incredible power of leverage. As he told me about his experience of building resilience in others, he said, "What has gotten you to where you are won't get you to where you need to be. It's important to learn from others who will give you insight that you don't currently have."

With that in mind, I am going to share six rewarding habits that will make a difference to your resilience and effectiveness as a leader:

1. The Rewarding Habit of Generosity

Winston Churchill once said, "We make a living by what we get, but we make a life by what we give." Generosity is all about giving in abundance to others, whether it's money, time, a chance, or investing in a larger cause. This also means helping others find meaning in their work, or giving them opportunities to maximise their strengths, or empowering them to innovate without fear of consequences. When you cultivate this habit of generosity in your life as a leader, you recycle goodwill, foster greater cooperation, and engender trust and loyalty in those you lead.

2. The Rewarding Habit of Reflection

Describing the power of this habit, Peter Matthews ✱ said, "As you mature as a leader, resilience comes from valuing the power of thinking over busyness." The late management guru Peter Drucker would absolutely agree. He said, "Follow effective action with quiet reflection. From the quiet reflection will come even more effective action." Taking the time to reflect is known to enhance performance more than gaining additional experience. It's all about consciously reviewing and considering our actions, beliefs, and assumptions for the purpose of learning. It's not about beating yourself up, but about growth. Regular reflection helps you understand your underlying assumptions and beliefs, which in turn guides you to better decision-making, especially when you step into new situations.

3. The Rewarding Habit of Mindfulness

Mindfulness is essential for any leader who wants to lead with greater purpose and authenticity. Mindfulness wakes us up to now. It stops us from sleepwalking through life, enables us to develop better mental habits and increased mental fitness, and unlocks our ability to connect with our best, authentic self as we seek answers to many daily challenges. It essentially has three components:

a) Being aware of what you are doing when you are doing it (breathing, walking, interacting, etc.).

b) Recognising any emotions and thoughts that may take you into the past or future.

c) Gently bringing yourself back to the present.

Research from the world of positive psychology, neuroscience, cognitive psychology, and performance science has shown that mindfulness can reduce stress, anxiety, pain, depression, and burnout, increase attention, and foster better sleep.

4. The Rewarding Habit of Gratitude

Gratitude plays an important role in our personal and professional lives. In essence, it is the emotion we feel after receiving something from another person, or from life, that is not earned, deserved, or intentionally sought after. Our brains are scanning for information all the time and often looking for threats, so when you develop the habit of gratitude, you are training your brain to see possibilities. I love the way Damon Hart✶ described this habit: "I've never had as much responsibility as I have at this point in my life. One of the things that helps me is maintaining an attitude of being grateful. I actually consider it a superpower. When I wake up, instead of saying, 'I have to x, y, z...', I say to myself, 'I get to do this... and I'm grateful.' It helps me maintain perspective and prevents me from always looking for greener pastures." Practicing gratitude daily is known to positively impact our well-being, relationships, happiness, self-control, and optimism.

5. The Rewarding Habit of Rest and Renewal

For every leader who desires to lead with more purpose and clarity, who wants to be able to prioritise better and be less stressed, who values productivity over hours worked, who wishes to avoid burnout, and who wants to live their best life, **making time for rest and renewal is critical.** This is all about the ability to pause, refresh yourself, and refill your energy so that you can continue to engage effectively with those around you.

Most leaders often take time to rest, but they don't know how to properly renew their energy. Many of the leaders I interviewed highlighted this as an important habit that keeps them sane, grounded, and energised. We all have different activities that we find restful and revitalising. Knowing what renews your energy and engaging in that as often as necessary is key to being at your best as a leader.

6. The Rewarding Habit of Vulnerability

Brené Brown describes vulnerability as "uncertainty, risk, and emotional exposure." It is the ability to share our lives with others in a way that creates psychological safety and helps build resilience in them. It is also about being comfortable not having all the right answers but learning how to inspire those answers in the people around you.

As a leader who wants to grow trust and loyalty in the team around you, you must allow vulnerability to feature as a way of being in your leadership. Lee Henderson✱ had a great reflection on this, "There's often a false expectation that comes with being a leader, that you have to know it all. Finding the confidence and self-acceptance to say that I'm not all I need to be, and I don't know it all, can be really powerful and build greater levels of trust in those around you." Martin Saurma-Jeltsch✱ echoes the sentiment, "Lots of leaders know they need to be vulnerable and yet don't do it. For me, one of the most liberating things I ever learned to do was say, 'That was my fault.'" And, despite what many leaders think, "It takes strength to be open and vulnerable," says Simon Robinson✱.

If you cultivate these six powerful and rewarding habits in your life, they will help you maximise your energy, your resilience, your attitude, your courage, and your impact. These are the sort of habits that begin to reinforce your internal structure, refine your moral character, and help you develop deep roots to navigate the storms and challenges of leadership.

Feed Your Mind with the Right Nutrition

You will notice that the six habits I focus on above have a lot to do with shaping your mental attitude. And that's because our mental habits drive our behavioural habits and have an impact on everything else, including the way we lead and interact with others.

When I was growing up, I had this strange belief that if I ate apple seeds, an apple tree would grow in my stomach. Believe it or not, I once ate some apple seeds and soil to see if anything would happen. Crazy, right? Of course, nothing happened. But here's the thing we all know, **what we put in influences what we get out**. Our physical diets influence the energy we bring to what we do each day. The same can be said of our mental diets. As the saying goes, "Garbage in, garbage out."

The late Earl Nightingale described our minds as a barren, fertile field and said, "Whatever you plant in it will grow." If you plant seeds of doubt, worry, greed, scarcity, and fear in your mind, then you will reap the fruit of anxiety, burnout, and distress in your life. But if you plant seeds of hope, courage, and excellence, then you will reap the fruit of vibrance, productivity, and empowerment in your life and that of the people around you.

Thanks to all the advances in neuroscience, we know that our thoughts create neural pathways that are strengthened over time and create habits that direct our destiny. It's no wonder that for most of the leaders

I interviewed, reading and reflection is a big part of their lives. They want to feed their minds with the right nutrition and practice mental gardening. "I'm always buying books, reading books, and looking for ways to constantly improve myself and add to my personal growth," said Timothy Lauren✶.

I strongly advise you to integrate the six rewarding habits outlined above into your personal leadership philosophy and life plan. Make it a habit to feed your mind with the right nutrition and reap the benefits of increased positive energy and impact in the way you live and lead.

QUESTIONS FOR REFLECTION

1. What leverage do you need to apply to achieve a breakthrough in your leadership effectiveness?

2. Carry out a mental diet inventory – what is the content of your mental diet, and how does it need to change to maximise your purpose, authenticity, and courage as a leader?

3. How can you integrate the six rewarding habits into your current approach to life and leadership?

CHAPTER 10

Nurture Empowering Beliefs

"You are no stronger than your belief system."

- T.D. JAKES

You might wonder why I refer to my personal leadership philosophy as 'Obi's Empowering, Limitless Story' and why I have memorised it. Well, it has everything to do with the Reticular Activating System (RAS) in the brain. The RAS is a bundle of nerves at our brainstem that filters out unnecessary information so the important stuff gets through. The RAS is the reason you buy a car and suddenly start seeing that model everywhere. It is the reason why you can tune out a crowd full of noisy people yet connect with someone calling your name. The RAS takes what you focus on and creates a filter for it. Here's why this is relevant. We are all telling ourselves stories all the time – those stories either empower us or cripple us.

When I was writing my first book, *The Magic of Monday*, I told myself the story that I was not good enough to write a book. That 'story', along with many other doubts and fears, crippled me for more than two years.

A big obstacle to developing and nurturing empowering beliefs is our inability as leaders to effectively deal with our doubts and fears and our propensity to blame circumstances rather than take complete responsibility for all areas of our lives.

I am pleased to say that now, through my empowering, limitless story, I have crafted a more empowering narrative about who I am and how I want to show up in the world, and this story helps me master the filters and direction of my thoughts.

CORE Leaders understand this and do the hard work of overcoming self-defeating behaviours by becoming more aware of their destructive and limiting beliefs, and intentionally nurturing empowering ones.

There are five primary ways to nurture empowering beliefs:

1. Bring beliefs to conscious awareness
2. X-ray your mind for the toxic weeds
3. Quell the doubts

4. Read your fears
5. Engage your inner coach

Bring Beliefs to Conscious Awareness

What do you believe about…

… the role of control in leadership?

… the ability of others to make the best decisions when they feel empowered?

… the need for compliance over autonomy in the workplace?

… the fact that the only way to succeed in business is to cross moral and ethical lines?

Do you believe that achieving your organisational goals is more important than '*how*' you achieve them?

Habits like reflection and journaling making a huge difference, as they help to surface some of the unconscious beliefs that drive the way you lead.

As you become aware of them, **ask yourself if your beliefs limit your impact and effectiveness, or if they enrich your impact and effectiveness.** If they enable you and others around you to thrive and achieve goals that serve the common good, then you know they are empowering beliefs. If they create and inspire passion, commitment, and innovation in others, then you know they are empowering, life-enriching beliefs.

X-Ray Your Mind for the Toxic Weeds

I have a confession to make. I am terrible at gardening. I can just about mow the lawn (even though my older boy does a better job than me). That said, I love to admire great gardens. I love our garden (and the people who help us look after it). I love what gardens can produce – flowers, trees, shrubs, colours, fragrances, etc. When you tend to them, they turn out beautiful. When you leave them to become overgrown, you create an absolute eyesore – a garden that is far below its potential.

One of the reasons that a garden must regularly be tended to is that entropy is natural. If you do not tend to it, the weeds will grow and suck the life out of the garden. That's life and that's nature. Weeds are a sign of neglect. And, "in the garden of our minds," it has been said, "limiting beliefs are the weeds."

In *The Big Leap*, Gay Hendricks describes how we all have an upper limit problem – an invisible ceiling beyond which we don't believe we can grow or change or perform at our peak. Some of the barriers and weeds include feeling fundamentally flawed, believing that success brings hidden burdens, or that we are committing a crime by shining or outshining others. Worry, criticism, blame, deflection, and arguments can all be signs that we are 'upper-limiting'.

What are your toxic weeds? Blame? Impostor syndrome? Judgmentalism?

Nurture Empowering Beliefs

You can discover this by asking questions like:

- Where in my life do I feel like I have compromised on my values and why?
- Where in my life do I feel like I have been holding back?
- Where in my life do I not feel like I am acting as my best self?

If you are not intentional about X-raying your mind for the limiting beliefs that are holding you back, you will find that you are subconsciously sabotaging your life and leadership.

Quell the Doubts

Ever since clinical psychologists Pauline Clance and Suzanne Imes first coined the term 'impostor syndrome', it has been acknowledged as a persistent reality in the lives of many leaders, including high achievers. It causes them to self-sabotage because they do not believe or feel they are as competent as others perceive them to be.

Impostor syndrome is the belief that you are inadequate, that you are a fraud, or that you will soon be exposed for who you really are. It puts an incredible amount of pressure and stress on many leaders, especially those playing the Ego Game. Biologically, it leads to higher levels of cortisol in the body and, for many leaders, it creates higher levels of anxiety, depression, and burnout. To overcome this as a leader, you need to take the time to explore your doubts, uncover the beliefs behind them, separate what is real from what is not with the help of trusted friends and advisors, and align yourself with a way of leading and serving others that makes it less about you and more about the contribution that your team, organisation, or community desires to make.

This is essential, because as a leader, the only way you can create an environment that inspires people to contribute their best thinking and their best selves is by removing the factors that cause them to doubt themselves and hold back. And this starts with yourself. Remember, you cannot give what you do not have.

Read Your Fears

Have you ever felt fear to the point that it crippled you? Maybe you had to deliver a high-stakes presentation to very important stakeholders? Maybe you took on a new role that would demand more from you than you had ever needed to give before?

I love these words from actor Will Smith in one of his films: "Fear is not real. The only place that fear can exist is in our thoughts of the future. It is a product of our imagination causing us to fear things that do not at present and may not ever exist. That is near insanity...

Nurture Empowering Beliefs

Now, do not misunderstand me, danger is very real, but fear is a choice. We are all telling ourselves a story."

Fear is a product of our imagination.

Karen Thompson Walker echoes this idea in her TED Talk "What Fear Can Teach Us". She says, "Read in the right way, our fears are an amazing gift of the imagination, a kind of everyday clairvoyance, a way of glimpsing what might be the future when there's still time to influence how that future will play out."

Rather than letting our fears cripple us, we can think of them like crystal balls that give us a 'potential' glimpse into the future. We shouldn't fear our fears, but read them, examine them, and use them as 'potential' signposts for ways we need to grow and action we need to take.

Engage Your Inner Coach

We all have that internal Jiminy Cricket, who says things that are helpful or unhelpful to us. For some, that internal voice can be absolutely vicious. We might think an internal self-rebuke motivates us to keep going or do better when we are not meeting our own standards, but it actually drains our energy.

If you're anything like me, you have also had to fight hard to retrain your internal narrative to not be so negative and hard on yourself.

As a leader, the quality of your self-talk influences

the quality of your beliefs as well as the way you show up and interact with others. If you want to maximise your energy, increase your impact, and build resilience, you need to take responsibility for the quality of your self-talk, making sure it's in line with your life vision and purpose.

This is where your leadership philosophy and life plan come into play. Used intentionally, they can shape and reinforce an internal narrative that is truly empowering, liberating, and refreshing.

Now you probably also understand why I have memorised my empowering, limitless story. I choose to be intentional about having a different narrative that guides my self-talk at a subconscious level.

Take Full Responsibility

To nurture empowering beliefs as a leader, you have to be committed to taking full responsibility for your life and attitude, no matter the circumstances.

Someone who knew this principle intimately was neurologist and psychiatrist Viktor Frankl, who survived the holocaust. He spent three years in the concentration camps of Auschwitz and Dachau. "We who lived in concentration camps can remember men who walked through the huts comforting others, giving away their last piece of bread. They may have been few in number, but they offer sufficient proof that everything can be taken from a man but one thing: the last of the human freedoms — to choose one's attitude in any given set of circumstances, to choose one's own way."

Responsibility can never be taken away from you without your permission.

Interestingly, the opposite of taking responsibility is blame, and there is far too much of it in organisations. In *You Don't Need a Title to Be a Leader*, Mark Sanborn tells the amazing story of Matthew 'Mattie' Stepanek. Mattie was born in 1990 in the US. By the time he was 13, he was already a *New York Times* bestselling author, an award-winning speaker, and had achieved a first-degree black belt in a form of martial arts known as Hapkido.

If any of that sounds impressive, get this – he achieved all of that despite having a genetic neuromuscular disorder known as dysautonomic mitochondrial myopathy, which meant he was eventually confined to a wheelchair. Even though Mattie very sadly died before his 14th birthday, he was one of those extraordinary individuals who already demonstrated a strong internal core at such a young age and refused to blame his circumstances or let them control his destiny.

I love the way George Bernard Shaw, the Irish playwright, puts it, "People are always blaming their circumstances for what they are. I don't believe in circumstances. The people who get on in this world are the people who get up and look for the circumstances they want, and if they can't find them, make them."

Blame is toxic, and a lot of leaders foster a blame culture instead of one of personal responsibility.

Taking full responsibility for our lives, our leadership, and the results we are getting is not easy. And yet, the more responsibility you take for your life, attitude, mindset, and leadership, the more you will find the power to create the life and leadership legacy you long for.

QUESTIONS FOR REFLECTION

1. What doubts are you plagued with? In what ways are they holding you back? What is the truth, and what choices can you make to ensure that you're able to focus on contributing with confidence as you lead?

2. What are some of the fears that limit your effectiveness as a leader? What could they be telling you about the mental and moral character muscles that you need to develop? What could they be telling you about the action you need to take to stop your fears from becoming a reality?

3. In what areas of your life and leadership do you need to take full responsibility?

CONCLUSION

Walk the Talk

*"If your actions inspire others to dream more,
learn more, do more and become more, you are a leader."*
- JOHN QUINCY ADAMS

We have covered a lot of ground, and our time together is fast coming to an end. I am hopeful that you have made the decision, or reaffirmed your decision, to be the sort of leader who truly leads well, complementing performance character with moral character. I am hopeful that this isn't the end for you, but rather the beginning of an unwavering commitment to personal leadership mastery.

According to many research surveys, **one of the most desired qualities in any leader is integrity.** Why? People want leaders who they know will treat them well. People want leaders who they know will use their power and influence for the common good. People want leaders who they know are ethical and will do the right thing, no matter who is watching.

Ultimately, people want leaders who walk their talk, who live by their values, who do what is right no matter the cost.

As Henry Cloud highlights in his book *Integrity: The Courage to Meet the Demands of Reality*, leaders who walk their talk and live with integrity have the ability to:

- Create and maintain trust in a way that wins people's hearts and minds
- Stay grounded in what is true
- Work in a way that gets results and finish well, thus reaching meaningful goals
- Embrace, engage, and deal with the negative realities of life and end up resolving, transforming, or transcending them

3 Things You Must Do in Order to Walk Your Talk

It's one thing to know your values. It is another thing altogether to live every day in congruence with those values. If you want to lead with purpose, authenticity, and courage, then you need to walk your talk and that means you must:

1. Accept that Your Life and Your Decisions Matter

Your decisions as a leader matter, especially in those inevitable moments when you face the difficult decisions of what to do at work, at home, in relation to customers, in relation to employees, in relation to stakeholders. If you're unclear about who you are and what you stand for, you will compromise when it counts. You will make decisions that you regret. You will abuse your power and use it for self-interest rather than to truly serve others.

2. Confront Any Conflict in Values

This doesn't mean you need to have the same priority of values as those you lead or the organisation you are part of, but it does mean that your values need to be aligned. If you value people, if you value service, if you value diversity, you need to confront any conflicts in those values or change your environment.

3. Know Your Purpose

You need to know and be connected with the purpose for your life and the purpose for your organisation. When you know your purpose, your why, you will be less inclined to waste time playing the Ego Game.

As we get ready to part ways, I have three final tips to encourage you to make the most of your ongoing journey of growth and development as a CORE leader.

Tip 1 – Commit to Mastery

Leading well, developing a strong core, and becoming a CORE Leader isn't a one-off event, rather it is an ongoing commitment to mastery.

"Mastery is a mindset," says Dan Pink, author of *Drive*. "It requires the capacity to see your abilities not as finite, but as infinitely improvable."

If you want your new approach to leadership to make a difference, not just in the short term, but for the rest of your life, then you need to commit to mastery – mastery of character growth, mastery of an empowering leadership philosophy, mastery of a compelling life plan.

Commit to seeing more potential in your people than they can see in themselves. If you are committed to mastery, you will always be on the trajectory of growth.

Tip 2 – Carve Out Specific Time

Building a strong character and developing a strong CORE does not happen by accident. It happens intentionally.

If you haven't already done so, allocate specific time slots in your calendar when you will work on your leadership philosophy and life plan, and then dedicate time to regular review.

One of the mantras I have adopted over the years (which helps me more than 90% of the time) is, "What gets scheduled gets done."

By committing to an ongoing journey of mastery and carving out specific time to top up your personal 'oxygen' tank, you are already demonstrating the strength of character that will make a significant difference to the way you lead.

Tip 3 – Commit to Going Deep

These words from Jim Rohn have stuck with me ever since I heard them more than 15 years ago.

> "Work harder on yourself than you do on your job because success is not something you pursue, it's something you attract by the person that you become."

I already know that you are someone who wants to have a positive impact on others and make a difference in your organisation, your family, your community, and our world. Otherwise, you wouldn't have picked up a copy of this book. You want to grow as a person of influence. Remember, **influence can do what command never can.** And influence, as we have established, is ultimately built on character.

The deeper and stronger your character, the more profound your influence will be.

So, commit to going deep.

EPILOGUE

"The real voyage of discovery consists not in seeking new landscapes, but in having new eyes."
- MARCEL PROUST

The ultimate goal of this journey has been transformation – seeing ourselves and leadership with fresh eyes. As we reach the end of our journey, I would like to reflect on these words from the late Mother Teresa:

"People are often unreasonable, irrational, and self-centred.

Forgive them anyway.

If you are kind, people may accuse you of selfish, ulterior motives.

Be kind anyway.

If you are successful, you will win some unfaithful
friends and some genuine enemies.

Succeed anyway.

If you are honest and sincere,
people may deceive you.

Be honest and sincere anyway.

What you spend years creating, others could
destroy overnight.

Create anyway.

If you find serenity and happiness,
some may be jealous.

Be happy anyway.

The good you do today will often be forgotten.

Do good anyway.

Give the best you have,
and it will never be enough.

Give your best anyway.

Epilogue

In the final analysis, it is between you and God.

It was never between you and them anyway."

If I may be so bold, I would like to add a line:

"Becoming an inspiring, engaging, and transformational leader is hard work. Become one anyway."

We have had quite a journey together. I am sure that you have gone to some very uncomfortable places that have challenged you to your very core, but I also hope that you are now convinced that this is the right way to be, live, and think when you call yourself a leader.

Let's rewind and revisit the realisation that I shared with you at the beginning of this book:

When life squeezes you and the pressure is on, what you're like on the inside will come out.

My desire in writing this book has been to challenge, inspire, and rouse you to live and lead more purposefully, more authentically, more courageously, and more effectively than you ever thought possible. So much so that, as you face the inevitable challenges, demands, and stresses of life (all the volatility, uncertainty, complexity, and ambiguity), what is on the inside will be something you can absolutely be proud of. This requires stepping back and courageously looking deep within yourself, at your life, your values, your worldview, your beliefs, your habits, and your character. It also means committing to internal workouts, intentionally crafting or re-crafting your life plan and leadership philosophy, and dedicating yourself to ongoing personal leadership mastery.

When you do that, not only can you call yourself a CORE Leader, you will know, with certainty, that you are one of the many inspiring, engaging, and transformational leaders making our organisations, our communities, our countries, and our world a better place for all. A leader who remains confident, resilient, courageous and who stands tall, even when the storms of life and business and ethics come their way. A leader who knows how to maximise their energy, increase their impact, and build their resilience.

I once heard that it is nearly impossible to rise above how we view ourselves. Our sense of identity and self-image drives our behaviour at such a fundamental and deep level. So much so that even when people are placed in correctional facilities, a place meant to seriously curb and change behaviour, it often does the opposite. If how people view themselves is the ultimate driving force of their behaviour, environmental changes only have a limited impact.

The same is true as a leader. This is deep work. It is about embracing an identity that will change things at a deep level for us.

Therefore, I encourage you to embrace and internalise the identity of a CORE Leader as set out in this book.

> **A CORE LEADER**
>
> … is committed to playing the Service Game
>
> … relates to others in a way that unleashes the best of their motivation, passion, creativity, and energy towards a worthwhile goal
>
> … puts in the hard work of leading from the inside out
>
> … has clear, compelling and congruent values
>
> … lives with an optimistic worldview
>
> … cultivates rewarding habits
>
> … nurtures empowering beliefs
>
> … is committed to living out stewardship as the heart of their leadership
>
> … embraces and pursues moral character as the currency of their leadership

This is the sort of leader who influences others for the better. It is the sort of leader who wins hearts and minds. It is the sort of leader who makes our world a better place.

Our world desperately needs more leaders like this. There's no question about it. The time is ripe. The time is upon us. The time is now.

Growing in your impact and effectiveness is not simply about acquiring new skills and competencies, but also embracing the character growth and deeper sense of identity required to lead in a way that is forever purposeful, authentic, and courageous.

Here's to living a life and leaving a leadership legacy that truly counts.

Here's to maximising your energy, increasing your impact, and building your resilience.

Here's to being a CORE Leader!

ACKNOWLEDGEMENTS

This book represents my passions and beliefs about the most inspiring and effective way to lead, and yet so much of what I believe and know has been influenced by many fantastic mentors who have spoken into my life, directly and indirectly, over the years. Too many to remember and yet there are some that absolutely stand out.

I'm grateful to Jon Flay, who probably ignited my passion for leadership and personal mastery when he gave me a copy of Stephen Covey's book, *The 7 Habits of Highly Effective People*. I think he gave it to me simply to inspire me to give my absolute best in my 'A' Level exams all those years ago. Little did he know that the book would be a catalyst for a much greater purpose and vision in my life.

I'm also grateful to all the leaders who I enjoyed hours of conversations with as we discussed and shared ideas about the impact of good and bad leadership, the importance of personal mastery, the challenge of burnout, and the path to resilience. Thank you for allowing me share some of your insights and stories in this book. Those leaders are:

Amadou Diallo
Amri Johnson
Andrew Agerbak
Andy Ayim
Avron Epstein
Charles McLachlan
Charles Sekwalor
Christoph Baeumer
Damon Hart
David Bang
David Smith
Devon Symister
Duncan Forbes
Emma Sexton
Femi Omere
Frank Vorrath
Gemma Hiett
Gilles Acogny
Gordon Steward
Hannah Martin
Helen Cresswell
Herman Stewart
Hilda Hegarty
Ian Joseph
Ian Wright
Jess Mullinger
Jo Ferreday
Joe Mamone
John Heard
JP Perraud
Julia Tybura
Katarzyna Marczewska
Kim MacGillavry
Lee Hendersen
Lily Manoharan
Lindsay Bridges
Luke Manning
Martin Saurma-Jeltsch
Mathias Lingnau
Matt Ovenden
Max Ward
Melanie Eusebe
Melissa Ribeiro
Melonae Thomas
Muriel Wan Antwerpen
Niki Frank
Nikki Craig
Nikola Hagleitner
Ommo Clark
Pam Roberts

Acknowledgements

Paul H. Graham
Peter Matthews
Sakshi Jawa
Simon Robinson
Stephen Howard
Teresa Hickman
Thiruselvaam Mateen
Timothy Lauren
Vivian Osayande
Wendy Cartwright
Yves Tournier

I'm grateful to Toye Oshunbiyi, Sandy Willoughby, and Stephen Howard, who read an earlier version of the manuscript and gave me some incredible feedback and input to strengthen it. To all three of you, your way of leading is inspiring to me and it was a joy to share this with you.

I'm also grateful to my Editor, Ine De Baerdemaeker of PostScripting, who helped me get rid of all the rough edges to create something that would be of tremendous value to leaders all over the world.

Finally, I am excited to thank my wife, Peju. Her unfailing support and words of encouragement and challenge call me to be someone who not only talks the talk but walks the walk. I'm forever grateful for our partnership.

BONUS SECTIONS

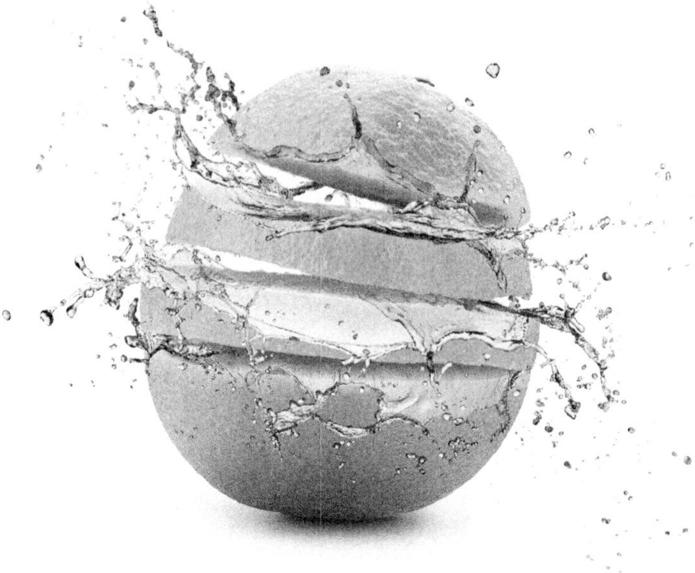

CRAFTING YOUR LIFE PLAN AND LEADERSHIP PHILOSOPHY

If you don't currently have a written life plan and leadership philosophy, then I strongly recommend that you start working on them by doing the following:

1. Visit www.coreleaders.co.uk/assessment to take our CORE Leader assessment. You will discover where you most need to focus your attention as you grow and strengthen your internal core.

2. Reflect on what you would want to be remembered for by your family, loved ones, friends, business partners, and colleagues. Based on the themes of these legacy statements, outline your most significant values.

3. Review the six rewarding habits described in Chapter 9 and consider what difference these could make to the way you live and lead. How can you integrate these habits into your current approach to life and leadership?

4. What do you believe is your current impact or influence on others? In times of stress, what beliefs limit your effectiveness? In challenging times, what beliefs help you to remain resilient?

5. Review the questions on pages 105/106. What do they reveal about your beliefs about people, about

governance, about life, about control, about leadership? What do they reveal about the strength of your moral character muscles?

6. The life categories that I focus on in my life plan are spiritual health, personal thriving, marital intimacy and connection, purposeful fathering, family and social connections, vocational excellence, financial health and stewardship, and Christian ministry. What categories most resonate with you? What CALM goals could you focus on in each of these categories to maximise your sense of fulfilment, purpose, and impact?

7. Revisit your answer to the question in Chapter 2: "What does leadership mean to you?" Considering everything you have read; how would you describe your leadership philosophy now?

THE PERSONAL MASTERY ACADEMY

Now that you've discovered the path to becoming a purposeful, courageous, and resilient leader, would you like to go deeper?

If so, CORE Leaders International's Personal Mastery Academy can help.

Through the Personal Mastery Academy, you will be able to:

- Access video resources to explore the ideas from this book in more detail
- Join a growing community of leaders from all over the world who are committed to personal mastery, leadership excellence, transformed lives, and a better world
- Receive personalised coaching to implement and integrate personal mastery skills into your leadership (VIP Level)
- Experience a full Personal Mastery MOT (VIP Level)
- And so much more…

Visit www.coreleaders.co.uk/personalmasteryacademy to find out more.

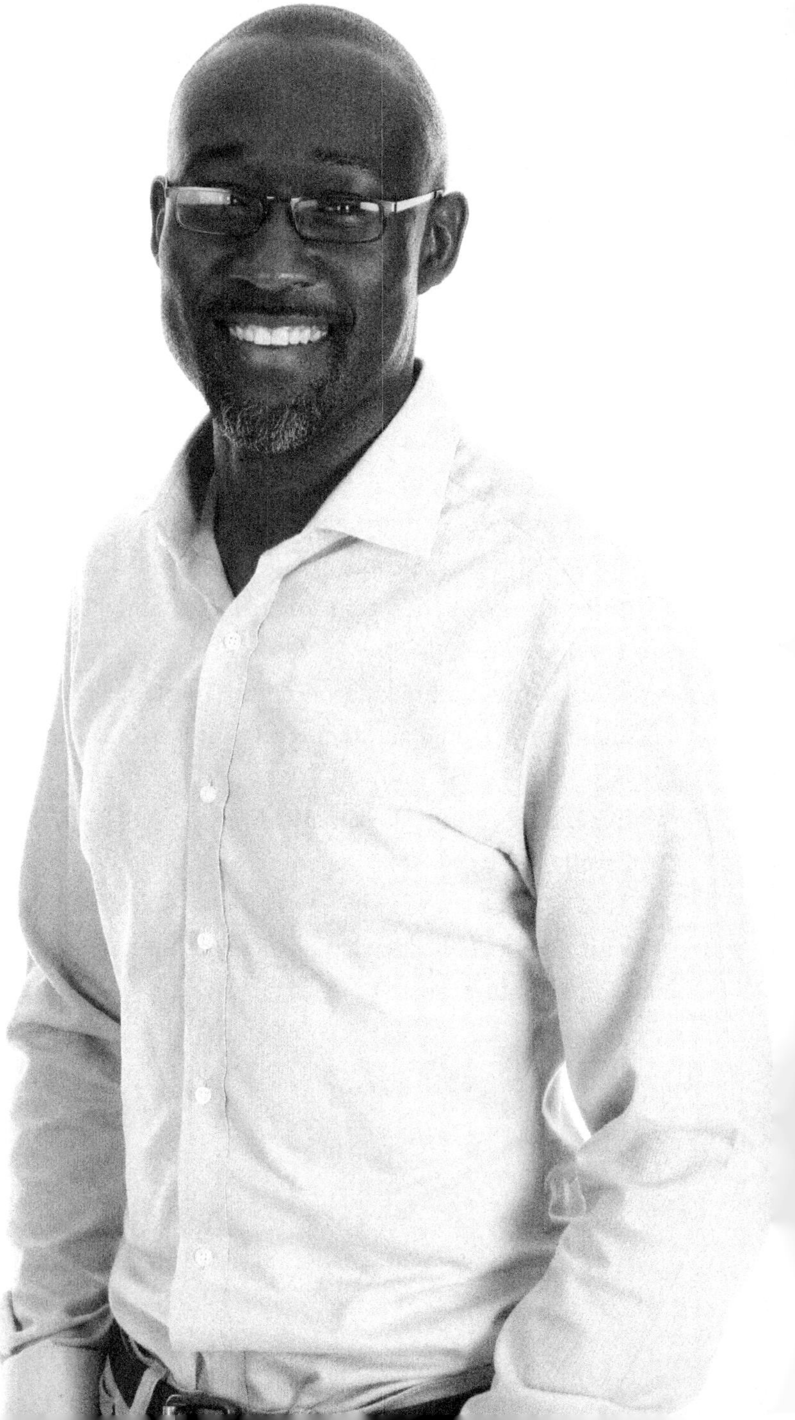

ABOUT THE AUTHOR

OBI ABUCHI is the founder and CEO of CORE Leaders International, a consultancy obsessed with helping leaders grow in personal mastery. He is also a transformational speaker and the author of *The Magic of Monday*.

He has worked with, trained, and coached leaders in corporate giants like Shell, Deutsche Post DHL, and Tesco to improve performance by redefining and shaping how they engage and inspire their people.

Through compelling and vulnerable stories, deep insights, boatloads of energy, and resilience coaching, Obi equips leaders to overcome self-sabotage in their leadership, know what they stand for, build moral character, hone their leadership philosophy, and achieve personal mastery so they can lead more purposefully, more authentically, more courageously, and more effectively than they ever dared to believe.

Obi's keynote topics include:

- Live and Lead from Your CORE™
- Unleash the Magic of Monday
- Winning F.A.S.T.E.R.
- Break Through Your Fear

www.obiabuchi.com
www.coreleaders.co.uk

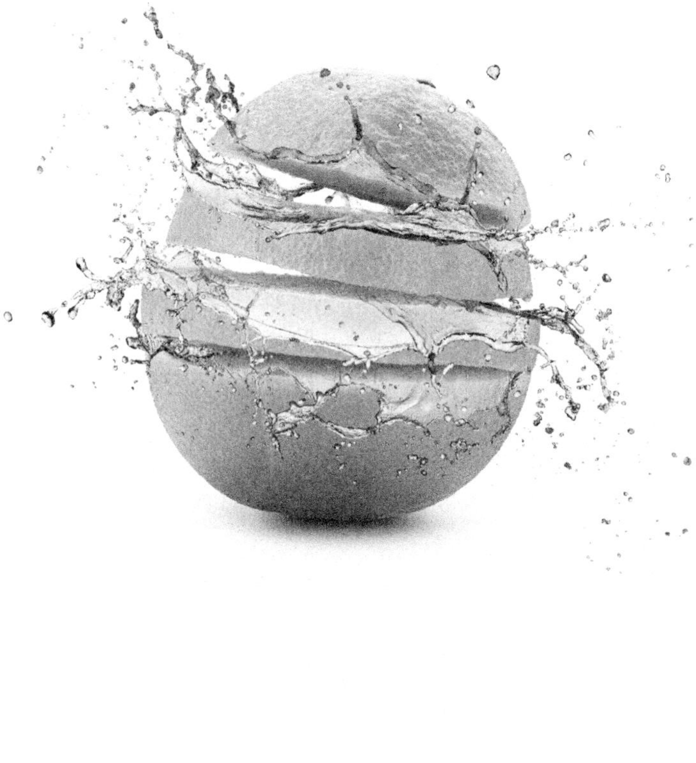

REFERENCES

Introduction
- p.53, Five Levels of Mental Toughness, Steve Siebold, *177 Mental Toughness Secrets of the World Class*: London House Press, 2010
- Oriah House Dreamer, *The Invitation*, 1999

Chapter 1
- "Enron and the Culture of Greed": https://www.nytimes.com/2002/01/23/opinion/enron-and-the-culture-of-greed.html
- Gallup State of the Global Workplace 2018 Report
- Mental Health Foundation's 2018 study undertaken by YouGovReport 2017
- Good Chiefs look after their family and spouse, Rhymer Rigby, April 29, 2015: https://www.ft.com/content/345e-4a9c-e759-11e4-8e3f-00144feab7de
- Byung-Chul Han, *The Burnout Society*: Stanford Briefs, 2015

Chapter 2
- Stephen R. Covey, *The 7 Habits of Highly Effective People*: Franklin Covey, 1998
- Marcus Warner and Jim Wilder, *Rare Leadership: 4 Uncommon Habits for Increasing Trust, Joy, and Engagement in the People You Lead:* Christian Art Publishers, 2017
- James C. Hunter, *The Servant*: Crown Business, 2012

Chapter 3

- p.77, Eckhart Tolle, *The Power of Now:* Hachette Australia, 2018
- p. 118, Pericles quote – As quoted in *Flicker to Flame: Living with Purpose, Meaning, and Happiness* (2006) by Jeffrey Thompson Parker,
- 'What would you say…' facts taken from: Peter H. Diamindis, *Get Abundance: Why Your Future is Brighter Than You Think:* Simon & Schuster Audio / Nightingale-Conant, 2015
- p.85-86, Jim Collins, *Good to Great*: Collins, 2009
- p.74, The Sage Perspective, Shirzad Chamine, *Positive Intelligence: Why Only 20% of Teams and Individuals Achieve Their True Potential and How You Can Achieve Yours*: Greenleaf Book Group Press, 2016
- Shawn Achor, *The Happiness Advantage*: Virgin Books, 2011
- p. 20, Charles Duhigg, *The Power of Habit*: Random House Trade Paperbacks, 2014
- Bruce Lipton, *The Biology of Belief*: Hay House Inc, 2016
- Shad Helmstetter, *What to Say When You Talk to Your Self*: Pocket Books, 1992

Chapter 4

- Raj Sisodia, David B. Wolfe, Jag Sheth, *Firms of Endearment: How World-Class Companies Profit from Passion and Purpose*: Pearson Education, 2014
- Peter Block, *Stewardship: Choosing Service Over Self-Interest*: Berrett-Koehler, 2013

References

Chapter 5
- Jim Loehr with Caren Kenney, *Leading with Character*: Wiley, 2020
- Erwin McManus, *Chasing Daylight*: Thomas Nelson Publishers, 2006

Chapter 6
- The Lesson of the Butterfly: https://paulocoelhoblog.com/2007/12/10/the-lesson-of-the-butterfly/
- How does a caterpillar turn into a butterfly? https://www.scientificamerican.com/article/caterpillar-butterfly-metamorphosis-explainer/
- Daniel Harkavy and Michael S. Hyatt, *Living Forward: A Proven Plan to Stop Drifting and Get the Life You Want*: Baker Books, a division of Baker Publishing Group, 2016
- Greg McKeown, *Essentialism: The Disciplined Pursuit of Less*: Virgin Books, 2014
- 7 Different Types of Strength and Their Benefits: https://www.acefitness.org/education-and-resources/professional/expert-articles/5495/7-different-types-of-strength-and-their-benefits/

Chapter 7
- Ayn Rand, *Philosophy: Who Needs It:* Blackstone Audio Inc, 2007
- Simon Sinek, *Start with Why*: Penguin Business, 2019

Chapter 8
- Walter D. Wintle, *Thinking*: Unity Tract Society, 1905
- Carol Dweck, *Mindset: The New Psychology of Success*: Ballan-

tine Books, 2008
- John Maxwell, *Failing Forward: Turning Mistakes into Stepping Stones for Success*: BookBaby, 2014

Chapter 9
- Brené Brown, *The Gifts of Imperfection*: Hazelden Information & Educational Services, 2010

Chapter 10
- The Reticular Activating System explained: https://medium.com/desk-of-van-schneider/if-you-want-it-you-might-get-it-the-reticular-activating-system-explained-761b6ac14e53
- Gay Hendricks, *The Big Leap*: HarperCollins, 2010
- Will Smith to his son, Qatar, in the movie *After Earth* (2013)
- "What Fear Can Teach Us", TED Talk by Karen Thompson Walker, https://www.ted.com/talks/karen_thompson_walker_what_fear_can_teach_us/transcript?language=en
- Victor E. Frankl, *Man's Search for Meaning: The Classic Tribute to Hope from the Holocaust:* Rider, an imprint of Ebury Publishing. 2004
- p.27-28, Mattie's Story, Mark Sanborn, *You Don't Need a Title to Be a Leader*: Doubleday, 2006

Conclusion
- Dr Henry Cloud, *Integrity: The Courage to Meet the Demands of Reality*: Harper, 2009
- Dan Pink, *Drive: The Surprising Truth about What Motivates Us*: Chungrim, 2011

Printed in Great Britain
by Amazon